Afrika Korps
AT WAR

Afrika Korps
AT WAR

1 ~ The Road to Alexandria

George Forty

IAN ALLAN *Publishing*

First published 1978
This impression 1998

ISBN — Ian Allan Publishing edition   0 7110 2579 7
ISBN — Vanwell Publishing edition   1 55068 068 4

© George Forty 1978/1998

Published by Ian Allan Publishing

an imprint of Ian Allan Publishing Ltd, Terminal House, Station Approach, Shepperton,
Surrey TW17 8AS.
Printed by Ian Allan Printing Ltd, Riverdene Business Park, Molesey Road, Hersham,
Surrey, KT12 4RG, England.

Code: 9809/A2

Contents

Foreword 7
Introduction 8
The Jerries are coming 14
Arrival in Africa 24
Organisation and Tactics 42
The Desert Fox 84
Rommel Strikes 98
Desert Living 114
Duels in the Sun 144
Honours Even 160

To the memory of all those gallant soldiers of the Deutsches Afrika Korps who fought and died far from their native soil in the desert wastes of North Africa.

Qui procul hinc, the legend's writ—
The frontier-grave is far away—
Qui ante diem periit;
*Sed miles, sed pro patria.**

* Last four lines of 'Clifton Chapel' by Sir Henry Newbolt (Reproduced here by kind permission of Associated Book Publishers Limited).

Foreword
General der Kavallerie a.D Siegfried Westphal

Tautly written and highlighted by many photographs, Lieutenant-Colonel Forty's *Afrika Korps at War* paints a vivid picture of the German soldiers who fought in North Africa from February 1941 to May 1943.

Hurriedly sent to help our Italian allies who had run into severe difficulties, the Afrika Korps' task was *strategically* defensive. Our role was to protect the southern flank of Europe, the 'soft underbelly' of the continent, to use Churchill's words. The Commander in Chief of the German and Italian forces, Field Marshal Erwin Rommel, endeavoured to fulfil his task with timely *tactical* offensives. His eventual failure was due to the strategic impossibility, in the long run, of transporting essential reinforcements over the Mediterranean to his divisions, and furnishing them with adequate aerial protection.

Throughout the book the author makes no secret of his respect for our soldiers and their gallant conduct. This respect is reflected wholeheartedly from the German side towards the British troops and forces of the Commonwealth. The campaign in North Africa in World War II was hard, bloody and demanded large and lamentable sacrifices. Standards of chivalrous conduct and morality on each side matched the highest traditions of both armies. This was a positive outcome from that bitter time.

Lieutenant-Colonel George Forty deserves the thanks of all old German soldiers in that he has given his fellow countrymen the view from the other side of the hill. This work should contribute to the final reconciliation of the former adversaries. For this reason alone I wish his book wide circulation.

Colonel Westphal seen talking to Rommel.

f. Westphal

Introduction

It is not unnatural for the soldiers of any nation to have a healthy respect for their adversaries. Indeed, it is always foolish to underestimate one's opponents even on the football field or the tennis court, so it is rank stupidity to do so on the battlefield. The British soldier has over the years developed, not only respect, but often affection, for his adversaries. This feeling is typified by some of Rudyard Kipling's poetry for example:

'We've fought with many men acrost the seas,
An' some of 'em was brave, an' some was not;
The Paythan an' the Zulu an' Burmese;
*But the Fuzzy was the finest o' the lot.'**

The wars which Kipling wrote about were fought by small armies of regular soldiers, whilst the great mass of the population stayed safely at home, not really involved to any great degree. It was not until World War I that large armies of conscripts were called upon to fight for their country and that mass destruction came to symbolise modern war. In these new circumstances it is difficult to imagine any soldier feeling affection for his enemy, indeed, the propaganda machines on both sides, did their best to bolster up the feelings of hatred. In general terms they were successful, and of all the armies which the Allies fought in World War II, one and one alone stands out as the exception to the rule. That army was Rommel's Deutsches Afrika Korps. Those who fought in the Desert still speak of the men of Rommel's army with the same mixture of respect and affection as perhaps the soldiers of Kipling's day did for the Fuzzy Wuzzy. But let me hastily add that there the similarity ends! Nothing could be less like a half naked, ill equipped native spearsman than the men of the Afrika Korps. They were truly professionals, well equipped and superbly led. They fought hard, with elan and dash, but on the whole fairly and with a chivalry that was reciprocated by their British counterparts. Desmond Young summed up the spirit in which the desert war was fought by quoting General von Ravenstein, commander of the 21st Panzer Division who was captured in November 1941:

'When I reached Cairo', he said, 'I was received very courteously by General Auchinleck's ADC. Then I was taken to see General Auchinleck himself in his office. He shook hands with me and said "I know you well by name. You and your division have fought with chivalry. I wish to treat you as well as possible".

Before I left Cairo I heard that General Campbell had been awarded the Victoria Cross. I asked and obtained permission to write to him. I still have a copy of my letter if it would interest you'.

The letter read:

Abbasia, 10 February 1942.
'Dear Major-General Campbell,

I have read in the paper that you have been my brave adversary in the tank battle of Sidi-Rezegh on 21-22 November 1941. It was my 21st Panzer Division which fought in those hot days with the 7th Armoured Division, for whom I have the greatest admiration. Your 7th Support Group of Royal Artillery too has made the fighting very hard for us and I remember all the many irons that flew near the aerodrome around our ears. The German comrades congratulate you with warm heart for your award of the Victoria Cross.

During the war your enemy, but with high respect.

Von Ravenstein'.

'Jock' Campbell was killed soon afterwards, when his car overturned near Buq-Buq. I do not suppose he ever received the letter. If he had, I think he would have appreciated it.*

I have so many people to thank for their help in generously providing me with photographs and reminiscences, that it is impossible to list them all here. However, their names appear throughout the book together with their stories and photographs, and I cannot thank them enough, because

* First verse of 'Fuzzy Wuzzy' from *The Barrack Room Ballads* by Rudyard Kipling. Reprinted by permission of the Executors of the Estate of Mrs George Bambridge and Doubleday & Company Inc.

* *Rommel* by Desmond Young.

without their help I could not have begun to tell the story of the Afrika Korps. Indeed, just as with my research on the Desert Rats, I have received so many offers of help that I have been unable to squeeze everything into one volume. Fortunately once again my publishers have agreed that the material is too interesting to discard and so it has been possible to divide it into two volumes. This first book deals with the initial rounds of the contest in North Africa, at the end of which the Afrika Korps found themselves right back where they started nine months previously. The remaining campaigns, ending with the final surrender in May 1943, will be covered in the second book, to be published shortly after this one. The Imperial War Museum has as usual provided me with invaluable assistance from their Photographic and Printed Book Departments. I must thank Doctor Haupt and his staff at the Bundesarchiv, Koblenz, who looked after me so well during my visit to their magnificent photographic library, and also my good friend Colonel Ted Bock and his charming wife, who entertained me when I visited Rommel's birthplace. I am particularly indebted to Colonel David Wilkinson of the Blues & Royals who, whilst serving as the British Liaison Officer at the German Armour

School at Münsterlager, obtained many of the reminiscences and other material for the book. He has, in addition, translated a great number of the stories for me for which I am eternally grateful. Also my eldest son, Simon, has nobly assisted with translations as well as acting as interpreter during our visit to Germany in the summer. Colonel Sievert Paulsen, the German Liaison Officer here at the Royal Armoured Corps Centre, has cheerfully translated an embarrassingly large number of letters for me for which I am much obliged. I must thank Herr Bernhard Bäter, Editor in Chief of the DAK magazine *Die Oase* for his kind assistance and finally General der Kavallerie a.D Siegfried Westphal for writing the foreword. As Rommel's Chief of Operations in Africa he was without doubt the best possible person to do this and I am greatly indebted to him for the trouble he has taken.

It has been a stimulating experience and a great privilege for me to meet and correspond with so many gallant and honourable men, whose brave exploits will long be remembered. *Heia Safari!*

Lulworth Camp, Dorset

George Forty
January 1977

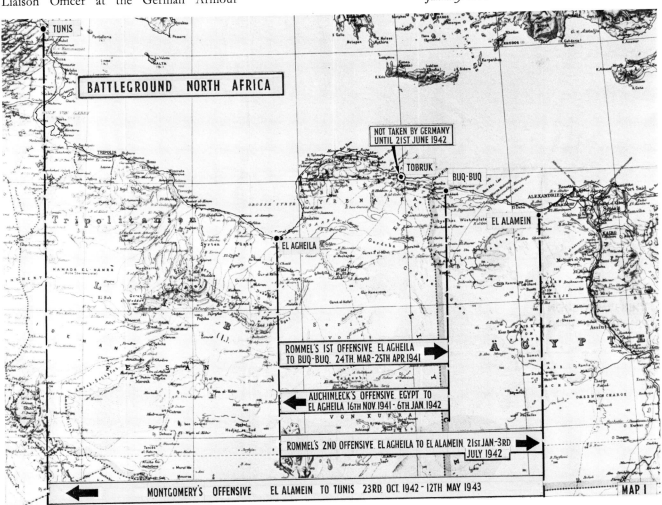

The Desert Fox

Above: The Fennec Fox.
/ *Zoological Society of London*

Together with that other equally famous denizen of the Western Desert the Jerboa, the name 'Desert Fox' has secured a unique place in history with its animal and human connections.

The Desert or Fennec Fox (Fennecus Zerda)

The Fennec Fox, or Desert Fox, is a diminutive species with a fluffy, creamy-coloured coat. This is not surprising, for most animals from desert regions are lighter in colour than their relatives from more hospitable areas. The tip of the nose is black, and the eyes are rather large, but the Fennec Fox's most remarkable features are its ears, which are huge. Again, this is understandable, for in the Sahara and Arabian Deserts where this animal lives, the day-time temperatures are so high that it is unable to hunt during daylight hours. It is only able to venture out at night, when keen hearing is all important and the big ears must pick up every minute sound. During the day the Fennec Fox remains in the shelter of burrows which it digs with its rather large paws. Towards evening it emerges and sits in the shade of stunted desert plants, protecting its head from the heat with its bushy tail. After dark it hunts, trotting briskly, but quietly, and often pausing to listen for insects, lizards, birds or desert rats upon which it feeds. Once food is detected, the fox disdains stealth and rushes straight at it. Any meat which cannot be eaten immediately is buried, for food is not so plentiful that it can afford to be wasteful. It then drinks at a waterhole, often meeting there the other Fennecs which use the burrows adjoining its own. Eventually it returns to rest again in its clean, snug, sleeping chamber, lined with dried plant material, feathers and hair. Should a Fennec Fox be surprised in the open, it burrows so rapidly that it almost seems to sink vertically into the ground.*

* Extract from *The Mammals* by Desmond Morris.

The Other Desert Fox

To some of us, however, the name 'Desert Fox' does not conjure up a diminutive wild creature but rather a single man—Erwin Johannes Eugen Rommel. Born in Heidenheim near Ulm on 15 November 1891, he joined the German Army in July 1910 and served with great distinction in the First World War as a young infantry officer, winning the '*Pour le Merite*', the German equivalent of the Victoria Cross, when, with a small force of about six companies, he captured the key Italian positions in the battle of Caporetto, taking nearly 10,000 prisoners and 81 guns. His meteoric rise to fame in the Second World War began with the almost unbelievable success which his Seventh Panzer Division achieved in France in 1940, when for the loss of only 42 tanks they captured 97,000 prisoners, over 450 tanks and armoured cars, 4,000 lorries and several hundred guns. This success led directly to his promotion to command the Deutsches Afrika Korps in February 1941. From then on until his eventual recall to Germany on the eve of the Axis collapse in North Africa in 1943, he displayed brilliant leadership in all phases of the war, building a reputation in his lifetime which few commanders have ever achieved. As Sir Winston Churchill said of him in the House of Commons in January 1942—'We have had a very daring and skilful opponent against us and may I say across the havoc of war, a great General'. After the end of hostilities in Africa Rommel's next major task was to strengthen the German defences along the French coast —the Atlantic Wall as it was called. Fortunately for the Allies he had neither the time nor the materials available to make it impregnable and thus could not prevent the 'D-Day' landings. A few weeks later, on 17 July 1944, the car in which he was travelling was attacked by a fighter aircraft and he was severely wounded. His skull was fractured in three places and he sustained numerous other wounds. On 20 July as he lay fighting for his life in a French hospital, the abortive bomb plot against Hitler took place. Some days afterwards one of the plotters, General von Stülpnagel called out Rommel's name as he came round from an operation—he tried to commit suicide as he was being brought to Berlin by the SS, but only succeeded in blinding himself—that was enough to implicate Rommel in the plot. But how could Hitler destroy Germany's national hero? Nothing happened for some two months while Rommel recovered from his wounds at his home in Herrlingen. Then on 14 October he was visited by Generals Burgdorf and Maisel. They brought Hitler's solution to the problem—if Rommel agreed to commit suicide by taking poison then he would be buried with full military honours, his family left alone and his good name preserved. If he refused he would be tried by a Peoples' Court and executed, whilst his family would be sent to a concentration camp. The choice was an obvious one for a man like Rommel. Two hours later the 'Desert Fox' was dead.

Below: Rommel, The Desert Fox, issues his orders./*Bundesarchiv, Koblenz*

The Desert Battlefield

The battlefields of the North African campaign were located not only in the arid, desolate wastes of the Western Desert, but also stretched along the entire Mediterranean coast, eventually reaching as far as the greener hills of Tunisia. However, it is still the Desert proper which is immediately brought to mind when one thinks about the great tank battles fought by the Afrika Korps. Here is how a British soldier—Charles Courtenay Forge, Paymaster of 7th Armoured Division, described the Desert to me:

'The Desert is not as most people imagine, a series of rolling sand dunes or flat sandy plains. The Desert is always changing its face, and in many places its scenery is interesting and in some aspects indeed beautiful. There are, of course, vast spaces of flat sandy plains and enormous areas of rolling sand-dunes, but there are many parts of the Desert which are broken and tortured by rocks and gullies, and parts where it is just stone and gravel, sometimes flat and sometimes undulating. In parts these stony areas are covered with a short scrub growing from one to three feet high and around which sand has been blown causing small hummocks which make travelling by any kind of mechanical transport extremely difficult. There are long escarpments of solid rock rising precipitously to several hundred of feet, and there are fantastically shaped hills of chalk and limestone around which rock and sand are intermingled, and which viewed from a distance give an impression of enormous ruined temples. There are wadis along which the water runs in the rainy season, and there are deep impressions which in bygone ages have been salt lakes. There are still many salt lakes in the Desert surrounded by *Sabakha*, the dry salt sand which formed at one time the bed of a now much smaller lake. And there are a number of oases where date palms and other fruits grow in abundance. As one enters the Desert along the coast road from Alexandria one sees miles and miles of desert, stretching away on both sides of the road, so barren, so almost frighteningly primitive, so incredibly hot, that it seems almost impossible that any human being, especially a white one, could exist there. Yet the great sand hills sheltered camps full of soldiers and airmen, who not only lived but worked and fought in them. The heat is really terrific, past all imagination; the air so burning and dry that it is difficult to breathe. The glare hurts, even with dark glasses to shade the eyes, and the endless miles of sand glitter as they shimmer in the heat.

But the Desert exerts a tremendous influence on people. You either love the

Deutsche Panzer vernichten indische Artillerie bei Sidi Omar

Carri armati distruggono le batterie dell'artiglierá indiana presse Sidi Omar

GENERAL DER PANZERTRUPPEN UND BEFEHLSHABER
DER PANZERGRUPPE AFRIKA

Desert or you hate it. There is no middle course. The Desert amply repays those who give it their love, for it has a fascination wholly its own. Nowhere in the world can one see such magnificent sunrises or sunsets day after day; and the varying colours of its landscape as the hours follow each other, changing from the pink flush of early dawn to a majestic purple as the sun rises higher in the heavens, and then to a beautiful gold as the evening draws on and the shadows lengthen, are such that one holds one's breath in sheer amazement that such beauty can come from the Desert; and the nights with their silence and their solitude underneath a galaxy of stars give to the mind a peace and contentment hard to find anywhere else. These are but a few of the rare gifts given by the Desert. But the Desert never forgives, to those who hate it the Desert can prove a relentless and implacable enemy, scorching them with its heat and blinding their eyes to its beauty with its fury and its dust. Even to those who have given it their love there come moments when they hate it, but this is only a passing phase, for the love once given can never be lost, for the Desert will always woo it back.

The Desert can be friend or foe. They who go to it must choose'.

Above: German tanks overrunning Indian artillery near Sidi Omar.
German Armour School, Munsterlager

Left: Erwin Rommel, June 1941. (Drawing supplied by F. Quick Esq.)/*A. Atkins*

Probably the best Italian AFV,
the Fiat-Ansaldo Autoblinda 41
(AB 41) seen here on patrol in a
native village. It had a crew of 4
—commander/gunner, two drivers
(one front, one rear) and a rear
hull gunner. Range 300 miles and
a top speed of 50mph.
/ *Bundesarchiv, Koblenz*

The Jerries are coming

February 1941 saw the British cock-a-hoop in North Africa. For the loss of only 500 killed, 1,373 wounded and 55 missing, they had destroyed an Italian army of four corps, capturing 130,000 prisoners, 400 tanks and about 1,300 guns. Although the British had achieved this almost unbelievable success so easily, it would be wrong to immediately write off the complete Italian army in North Africa as useless. It is true that the average Italian soldier had little 'heart for the war. Badly officered, badly equipped and desperately short of all modern weapons, they had many problems. This is how General der Kavallerie a.D* Siegfried Westphal, who served as Rommel's Chief of Staff in the Afrika Korps, described the Italians in North Africa in a lecture to the Anglo-German Association in April 1959:

'The Italian soldier was at a disadvantage compared with us as far as weapons, equipment, and other imponderables were concerned. He was neither equipped nor prepared for a war against a European opponent armed with the most modern weapons, because the Fascist regime had neglected the armed forces. The Army was particularly at a disadvantage in respect of tanks, anti-tank equipment, artillery and anti-aircraft defence. A considerable portion of the Army's guns was still composed of the booty collected on the collapse of Austria-Hungary in the autumn of 1918. Their wireless posts were not in a position to transmit or receive while on the move. There were no field kitchens,

and the rations were insufficient. Their industry was not equipped to meet the requirements of the armed forces during a war of long duration. It was therefore incomparably more difficult for our allies than for us. This has unfortunately not always been taken into account when judging their achievements. At any rate, I am convinced that we would also have been unable to achieve more success with such out-of-date and inadequate arms and equipment'.*

Given the right leadership the Italians fought bravely enough, for example, their tanks put in nine determined attacks upon the 2nd Battalion of the Rifle Brigade, whilst trying desperately to break through at Sidi Saleh in February 1941. Unfortunately for them the attacks were unco-ordinated and, although they penetrated as far as Battalion headquarters, they were stopped there and the 10th Italian Army could not escape its ultimate fate. At Nibeiwa Italian gunners continued to man their guns right up to the moment when British tanks over-ran their positions. However, what army could ever hope to win a strenuous desert campaign which had different menus for almost every rank from private soldier to general; where officers went into battle equipped with clean sheets, comfortable beds and motor caravans full of whores; whose commanding general (Graziani) retired first to a Roman tomb seventy feet below ground in Cirene and then left North Africa altogether and conducted

* a.D = Retired.

* Published in the RUSI Journal 1960.

his campaigns from the safety of the Italian mainland!

It was understandable, therefore, that a certain amount of friction was bound to exist between the Germans and Italians in North Africa. Rommel's policy of being well forward where he could personally see to control the battle was so different to that of his Italian contemporaries. But perhaps they had good reason to be cautious, as Desmond Young relates in his classic book on Rommel which I have read and re-read many times over the past twenty five years: 'When General Berganzoli ('Electric Whiskers') surrendered unconditionally on 7 February 1941, he was joined in captivity in Dehra Dun by more general officers than India had seen together since the 1911 Durbar'.

With the surrender of the 10th Italian Army the whole of Cyrenaica lay in British hands and the road to Tripoli appeared wide open whenever General Wavell chose to take it. Two months later, however, the situation had altered dramatically. Once again the enemy was back on the Egyptian frontier, Tobruk was under seige and such famous generals as Sir Richard O'Connor and Philip Neame, VC, together with the newly arrived GOC 2nd Armoured Division, Gambier-Parry, were all 'in the bag'. What had caused this sudden reversal of fortunes, which had all the belly dancers and bar-keepers in Cairo rushing for their German and Italian phrase books? The answer, although it may sound far fetched, was simply one man—Erwin Johannes Eugen Rommel. Few men ever become legends in their own lifetime, but Rommel did so and with such devastating

Above: British troops with two captured Italian 'tankettes' CV33/35. The CV33 had even thinner armour than the CV35 and was armed only with one 8mm machine gun whilst its sucessor had two, plus telescopic gunner's sights./*H. Martin*

Top right: Italian infantry in a sandbagged desert sangar. The light machine gun is the 6.5mm Breda Modello 30, which had a rate of fire of 450-500rpm. / *Bundesarchiv, Koblenz*

Bottom right: Italian gun crew firing a Breda 47/32 M35 anti-tank gun from a desert sangar. This gun was the standard Italian infantry anti-tank gun, which had a secondary role of providing close supporting fire. It could penetrate about 43mm of armour at 0° and 550 yards. / *Bundesarchiv, Koblenz*

thoroughness as to cause the British Commander in Chief, Middle East Forces, to publish a special order about him which read:

To: ALL COMMANDERS AND CHIEFS OF STAFF
From: HEADQUARTERS, B.T.E. AND M.E.F.

There exists a real danger that our friend Rommel is becoming a kind of magician or bogeyman to our troops, who are talking far too much about him. He is by no means a superman, although he is undoubtedly very energetic and able. Even if he were a superman, it would still be highly undesirable that our men should credit him with supernatural powers.

I wish you to dispel by all possible means the idea that Rommel represents something more than an ordinary German general. The important thing now is to see to it that we do not always talk of Rommel when we mean the enemy in Libya. We must refer to 'the Germans' or 'the Axis powers' or 'the enemy' and not always keep harping on Rommel.

Please ensure that this order is put into immediate effect and impress upon all Commanders that, from a psychological point of view, it is a matter of the highest importance.

(Signed) C. J. AUCHINLECK
General.

Whether or not one agrees on the need to publish such an order, there can be no doubt that Rommel's presence had caused a major change in fortunes to the British. It was all too apparent to the front line troops of the 2nd Armoured Division, as they recoiled in front of his first onslaught, that here indeed

was a very different kind of enemy. So let us take a closer look at the night of 31 March 1941, when Rommel began his initial three pronged advance into Cyrenaica. Here is how it was described by Paul Carell in the opening chapter of his evocative book *Die Wüsten Füchse*)

'A silent, pitch-black night shrouded North Africa. It was past midnight on the 31 March 1941.

In a depression among the sand dunes before El Agheila, on the western frontier of Cyrenaica, lay a British reconnaissance patrol. From the top of the dunes the two officers observed a fort through their night field glasses. For a long time they watched the enemy position in silence. Lieutenant Fred Miller, known to his friends as "Dusty", cocked his ear attentively in the direction of the Italian positions. He nudged his friend, Lieutenant James Clark. "I'll tell you something, Nobby, the war has stopped breathing". It was in fact, deathly still and the great silence of the night lay over the desert. It certainly seemed as though the war had come to a standstill—at least temporarily. No shouts from the sentries, no rattle of weapons, no noise of some rumbling truck, not a sound from the enemy lines.

Clark and Miller, with the driver and the wireless operator, formed the crew of a green-and-yellow camouflaged British armoured scout car which stood hidden among the high dunes. The rear right mudguard bore the emblem of the 7th British Armoured Division, a red jerboa in a white circle. The wits among the 11th Hussars, at the *thé dansants* at the Continental in Cairo, used to

say to the ladies: "Graziani's quarter of a million Italians took to their heels like a woman who has seen a mouse". They had run from the Egyptian frontier to Tripolitania, from Sollum to El Agheila, to the very spot where the scout car stood waiting to see whether the Italian would venture to fight back.

The 11th Hussars, who had exchanged horses for tanks, and with whom Clark and Miller were serving, was now attached to the 2nd Armoured Division. "The glorious 7th" was no longer at the front. It had been sent back to Cairo for a rest. Since the hurried transfer of British front-line troops from North Africa to Greece had very much weakened the reconnaissance units, "Nobby" and "Dusty" both well-trained intelligence officers, had joined the 2nd Armoured Division which was in the front line at that time facing the routed Italians. It was easy to see by Miller's lobster red face that he had not been very long in the sand and the sun. The 19-year old lieutenant had arrived a few days before by air from Cairo from the reserve battalion of the 11th Hussars. He was delighted to find his friend, James Clark there. Felton, the driver, had prepared their supper over a little fire in a sand-hole. He had thrown long strips of spaghetti from a blue packet into boiling water and opened a tin of preserved cherries with his bayonet. The four men proceeded to eat this diet which was strange indeed for the British. The noodles, parmesan cheese and preserved fruit were the loot with which they had stuffed their car on 7 February, the day Benghazi fell. While Clark, Felton and the wireless operator Corporal Farquhar, ate in silence, Miller began to ask questions. He confessed how much he regretted not having been present during the pursuit of Graziani's Italians between December 1940 and February 1941. In this hectic, victorious British advance in the North African Desert ten Italian divisions were routed; 130,000 prisoners were taken, 400 tanks and 1,200 guns captured. What a war! What a victory! And to have missed it! As soon as the men had wrapped themselves in their overcoats and crept under the truck, Clark stuck a Players in his mouth and began to tell a story which was common knowledge throughout the whole Army. The story of "Electric Whiskers" whom he had captured and for which feat he had won the MC "Electric Whiskers" was the subject of countless anecdotes in Cairo and London. It was the nickname given to the wiry little Italian Corps Commander, General Bergonzoli, in the Spanish Civil War and it had stuck to him here in Africa. His soldiers had christened him *"Barba Electrica"* because his red beard apparently gave off red sparks. No one really knew why this General had become popular on both sides of the line, but it was so. During the victorious British campaign in Cyrenaica it had become a sporting issue to capture *"Barba Electrica"*. After every victory, after each conquered town, the question was asked among the staffs and in the British newspapers: 'Have they caught "Electric Whiskers"?' But the little Italian General seemed to enjoy a charmed life. He lost every battle and in due course his entire Army Corps, but he himself escaped—from Sollum,

from Bardia, from Tobruk and from Derna. "But I got him in Benghazi", said Clark. "When I stuck my tommy gun through the window of his Fiat, he said to me: 'You got here a bit too quick today'. He looked tired. I took him to General O'Connor and was present at the interrogation. I shall never forget it. We asked him how he managed to escape so many times. *'Barba Electrica'* replied: 'When you surrounded Bardia in December, I slipped through your lines at night with a few of my officers. During the day we hid in caves and it took us five days to reach Tobruk. When Tobruk fell, I managed to make my way to Derna. But when that stronghold was beseiged by the Australians I drove along the coastal road to Benghazi. But now you've got me. You were too quick, that's all'."

In Benghazi, apart from him, the British had captured half a dozen generals. The Bersaglieri General Bignani, the Artillery General Villanis, the Sapper General Negroni, the Tank General Bardini, General Cona and his chief of staff, General Guiliano. They simply waited for them. "I haven't seen so many Generals since the 1911 Durbar", General O'Connor remarked. The British were confident. Before long they would be in Triploi. It would be fun. The "Eyeties" always had good bases, they were said to go to war with every possible comfort. In Benghazi the British claimed to have captured a whole truck full of girls "For Officers only". What a lovely war! The armoured car crew wrapped themselves up tightly in their overcoats for the desert night was cold. Clark rolled over on his side. "Keep your

Below: Tanks of 7 RTR fly Italian flags after capturing Tobruk in January 1941./*4th Royal Tank Regiment*

eyes skinned, Dusty, that the Eyeties don't grab us". Then half-asleep he added: "And take care that the war doesn't start breathing again . . ."'

Lieutenant Clark certainly did not realise that in another couple of hours the war would start to 'breathe again' with a vengeance, because without his knowledge, a new ingredient had been added to the Desert war and that was the German Afrika Korps. Hitler, worried about the consequence of a complete Italian collapse in North Africa, had finally decided to send in small numbers of German troops to bolster up the Italians. Between 14 and 20 February 1941, advance units of the 5 Leichte (Light) Division, had been arriving in Tripoli. They were to be joined in early April by 15 Panzer Division. Together these two divisions, according to a directive issued from the Führer's headquarters on 19 February, were to be known as the "Deutsches Afrika Korps". Their commander was to be a Generalleutenant Erwin Rommel, who had distinguished himself commanding the 7th Panzer Division in the invasion of France in May 1940. His initial orders from Hitler were to plan no offensive action against the British. Once his force was complete he could then carry out limited aggressive acts, but his main job was to prevent the loss of further territory by the Italians. We shall, of course, be dealing with the arrival of the German forces more closely and will also look in detail at their famous commander, but for the moment to return to that Eleventh Hussar reconnaissance patrol outside El Agheila: . . .

'Lieutenant Fred Miller dozed in the silent night near El Agheila. All he could hear was the snoring of his comrades. At the moment the war began to "breathe" again.

The clank of tank tracks . . . Then silence and an oath. Fred Miller was on the alert, but there was no need for him to wake the others. Clark, too, was peering out from under the scout car. They lay on their bellies and stared ahead at mighty shadows which rattled as they moved. They heard shouts. "Tanks", whispered Miller, "German tanks". The monsters drove past 30 yards away in a southerly direction. "One, two, three, four, five . . .", Clark stopped counting. The sixth veered and made directly for them. "Move off", yelled Clark. The driver and wireless operator were already in the car. The self-starter hesitated. "Get cracking, man!" At last. The rattling shadow was almost on them as they drove off. The desert suddenly sprang to life, the shadows coming from all directions.

They reached the Mersa el Brega road, sped towards the Arab village with the white mosque on the heights. Dawn began to break on an historic morning. "German tanks to the south and on the coastal road", James Clark shouted to the commander of a reconnaissance unit of the 2nd Armoured Division, which lay in front of Mersa el Brega.

The news ran like wildfire through the unit.

They drove off in their Bren carriers but they did not get very far. Rommel had begun his first battle.

At 09.44 hours on 31 March 1941, the "recce" cars of the Stahnsdorf 3rd Recon-

Below: The crew of a British Bren Gun Carrier takes a close look at a monument erected by the Italians in commemoration of their capture of Sidi Barrani. */IWM*

Above: Piles of captured Italian rifles and machine guns, February 1941./*IWM*

naissance Unit near Mersa el Brega ran into an advanced "recce" unit of the 2nd Armoured Division. At 09.50 hours the first shells burst . . . The opening shots in Rommel's wild ride to Tobruk.

After the duel between the reconnaissance units which ended with the retreat of the British, the tanks of the 5th Panzer Regiment from Berlin-Wunsdorf under Lieutenant-Colonel Albrich attacked the actual Mersa el Brega position. Eight days before, during the storming of the desert fort El Agheila, the regiment had suffered its first casualties when one of its tanks drove over a mine, the first casualties of the Afrika Korps. That day they attacked again. Corporal Gerhard Klaue of No 8 Company from his turret spotted his first enemy, a camel which rushed like a wild thing towards the German armour. Was this some devilish stratagem of the "Tommy"? Presumably not. The beast sheered off and disappeared in a cloud of dust. The Panzers continued to advance but they could make no headway against the strongly held British position.

At 17.30 hours two German Stuka attacks on the British lines followed in swift succession. Heavy flak was brought to bear on the British artillery positions. The thermometer registered a hundred degrees. The infantry slowly felt its way through the undulating sand dunes. Then the first mines went up. "Sappers forward!" They planted their black flags and swept a path through the field. These black flags waving in the bright sunlight, pointed the way to the motorised infantry and the men of the 8th Machine-Gun Battalion. They attacked. The first men fell, but Mersa el Brega was taken—the desert gate to Cyrenaica.'

German Preparedness

As I have explained, once Hitler realised that the Italians would be unable to hold further British advances without assistance, he decided to send a German blocking force to North Africa to help them. Thus the Afrika Korps was born. Rommel then proceeded to get his forces into action so quickly after landing, that it must have seemed to the British Headquarters in the Middle East that Germany had been preparing for such an eventuality for some considerable time. In fact nothing could be further from the truth. To quote again from General Westphal's talk to the Anglo German Association:
'And now I want to deal with the question as to whether and to what extent Germany was prepared for a campaign in Africa. On this context I remember a small incident in 1938. I was at that time in the Operations Section of the General Staff in Berlin. One of my tasks was to justify the demands of the operational staff in the training, organisation and technical fields etc, to the other departments and offices of the High Command. I had therefore, to be a kind of "pike in a carp pond" as my Section chief, the late Field-Marshal von Manstein, put it. One day an officer of the Section who had to arrange for the provision of the maps which would be necessary in the case of a war came to me: he suggested that the existing supply of maps of the West, East and South-East should be

troops to North Africa. It had no time to make thorough preparations for this type of operations. Consequently, only the most necessary organisational and sanitary measures could be taken. It was equally impossible to accustom the troops gradually to the great heat and to change their training to prepare them for fighting in country providing no cover. The plans for the lines of supply also had to be made at very short notice. Moreover to begin with, troops as well as heavy equipment were all transported by sea. When, however, shipping losses piled up, all the transport of personnel was carried out by air only. All measures therefore had to be more or less taken ad hoc; experience could mostly only be gathered on the spot'.

Nevertheless, once the order had been given to send troops to North Africa, then as far as possible, the Germans got down to detailed planning in their usual methodical way. There was much to do. First of all the troops selected had to be medically examined to make certain that they were fit enough to serve in the desert. Next they had to be equipped with tropical uniforms—we shall see exactly what they received later—and their vehicles camouflaged with sand coloured paint. Training programmes had to be adapted to include subjects such as operating in wide open spaces, field hygiene, water discipline and so on. Special units to handle the vital supply of water had to be formed and trained. These were but a few of the problems, another was deciding on proper rations to suit the desert conditions. Bread and potatoes which formed the staple part of the normal European diet was considered unsuitable for North Africa. *"Zwieback"* (black bread in a carton) replaced white bread and legumes (peas and beans) the potatoes. As butter would go rancid quickly in the heat, olive oil and tinned sardines were substituted. The Italians were able to provide some food, such as cheese, cooking oil, coffee beans and marmalade. Also the famous —or should it be infamous—tinned meat, each tin stamped with the letters "AM". I have been unable to discover what this actually stood for, but it was known throughout the Afrika Korps as *"Alter Mann"* (Old Man) or *"asinus Mussolini"* (no translation needed!) The German rations were adequate if rather solid, but not as appetising as those of the Allies—so there was always great rejoicing when a British supply dump was captured and they could dine on bully beef, white bread and jam. Perhaps it was just that the grass always appeared greener on the other side of the fence, for many Desert Rats I have spoken to for their part, enthused about the Italian and German rations which they captured, maybe they should just have swapped Quartermasters!

augmented by a set for both Scandinavia and North Africa. One never knew what might happen. The absence of maps of Palestine had already proved a great disadvantage in the previous war and so on. Well, I rejected this suggestion immediately on my own initiative and met with the full approval of my superiors. None of us even dreamed of the possibility of ever having to wage war in the desert. It must be remembered that Germany then no longer had any possessions outside Europe, and for this reason we were not accustomed to think in all-round terms. I met that officer again three years later when I went to Libya and he was in charge of our transport in Italy. He soon reminded me of that conversation of ours. Not without triumph in his voice, he pointed out that he had been right. The German troops now had to make do with makeshift maps, the markings on which differed often by several kilometres from the real position. I had opportunity enough in the coming months to satisfy myself that this was correct. And whenever—as often happened—the bad maps were cursed, I always had rather a bad conscience. This small anecdote may serve to show that there had been no preparations of any sort in the German Army before the second World War for a possible campaign in a theatre of war outside Europe. As a matter of fact, as we shall see later, German troops landed in North Africa at the beginning of 1941 almost completely unprepared for their new task. All this should prove that it was almost a complete surprise to the German military command to have to send

23

Arrival in Africa

Another tank is loaded on board
a transport ship in Naples
harbour./*Bundesarchiv, Koblenz*

Above, top right: Farewell parade of an artillery unit on a wintery barrack square in Germany—it will be a long time before they see the snow and ice again. (The guns are 15cm howitzers)./*Brig P. A. L. Vaux*

Bottom right: German troops rest on the dockside before embarking on a troopship for North Africa./*IWM*

First to Land

The first German combat troops arrived at Tripoli harbour on 14 February 1941. They were personally inspected there by Rommel, who had landed, with various members of his staff, at Castel Benito airfield some fifteen miles south of Tripoli two days previously. After marching past in review the men of the 5 Leichte Division kept on going and reached Misurata, farther down the coast of Tripolitania, later the same day. Advance units of the divisional reconnaissance battalion (AA 3) moved on as far as Sirte, where they were ordered to remain in mobile reserve. It was about this time that Rommel, faced with the problem of making the British believe that his forces were too strong for them to attack, decided to have dummy tanks constructed. He wrote of this ruse in a letter home:

'To enable us to appear as strong as possible and to induce maximum caution in the British, I had the workshops three miles south of Tripoli produce large numbers of dummy tanks, which were mounted on Volkswagen and were deceptively like the original'*

On 19 February Hitler issued a directive announcing that from that date onwards the German forces in Africa under Rommel

* *The Rommel Papers* edited B. H. Liddell-Hart.

would be known as the Deutsches Afrika Korps (DAK). In addition, the directive went on to say that in order to reinforce 5 Leichte, a full Panzer division would be transferred to Tripolitania. This was to be 15 Panzer Division which began landing in late April 1941 and was complete by mid June.

The British gained their first positive identification of the presence of German troops in North Africa when, on 21 February, a pilot flying west of El Agheida, spotted an eight wheeled armoured car—an Sd Kfz 231 —which was unmistakably German.

First contact with the British was made on 24 February when Advance Unit Wechmar (namely AA3—5 Leichte's reconnaissance unit) bumped into two troops of British armoured cars and a troop of Australian anti-tank guns. In the engagement which followed the British lost one armoured car, one truck and three scout cars, one of which was towed away by the Germans.

Journey to Africa

How did the German soldiers reach North Africa? The first part of the journey was normally overland to Italy and thereafter, there was a choice of transportation by sea or by air. Werner Susek moved with 190 Artillery Regiment by sea, and he wrote of the journey:

'We left Wahn, near Cologne, on 27 October

1941 and spent a few weeks at Bagnoli near Naples. We were then shipped to Benghazi and reached there finally on 24 November. There were two troop transports, with two destroyers and a Heinkel protecting us. Two days out we were attacked by British bombers, but there was no damage. Then our ship developed engine trouble and had to stop at Crete, so it was a long journey'.

Karl Susenberger, going out as a reinforcement to 104 Panzer Grenadier Regiment went by air and described his journey thus: '*Brindisi, 22 April 1942*
It was about 2300 hours when our transport arrived at Brindisi. We immediately disembarked and were taken to our quarters. It was a barracks that had originally been Italian. We were told on parade the next morning that we would be staying here for a few days. We were advised not to go out alone because of attacks which had occurred on single soldiers. We took heed of this warning, but everything stayed peaceful. After about a week, early one morning, we were taken to the aerodrome, now this was it. The many JU52s that would fly us to Africa made an impressive sight—there must have been about thirty five in all. We were divided into groups of eighteen and were taken to the plane, life jackets were handed out and then we had to get in. I had a window seat so I could easily see what went on. Who would

27

have thought nine months ago whilst training as radio operators in Brunswick, that we would be flying today to Africa. No one! The machines taxied to the runway and off we went towards Africa, for all of us it was a great experience, above all it was a fantastic sight to see all the machines in the air. After about four hours we landed in Crete. The aerodrome lay immediately beside the sea—inviting a quick bathe. There were also wonderful oranges. I've never seen the like of such oranges even in Italy and Siciliy. After about four days we were told to make ready as the next day we would fly on to Africa.

On to Africa

It was 6 May 1942 when we got back into the JU52s in order to fly on to our final destination. This time we had fighter protection—consisting of two ME110s, a bit stingy for a formation of thirty five planes. As the formation neared the African coast there was a sudden alarm call—"air attack—enemy fighters behind!"

Already the first tracers were whizzing through the air. Our fighters and rear-gunners took up the fight, but in spite of this the Tommies shot down three JU52's, three machines filled with our comrades who would never reach Africa. After this fore-taste we could guess what awaited us there'.

Lt Ralph Ringler who also joined 104 Panzer Grenadier Regiment kept a detailed diary of his personal journey out to Africa in August 1942. At that time the regiment was located

just behind the front line at El Alamein, it had come to Africa in March 1941 as the 15th Kradschützen (Motor-cycle) Battalion and fought throughout Rommel's initial campaign at Capuzzo, Sollum and Halfaya Pass. In May 1941 they had attacked Tobruk and by December 1941 their fighting strength was reduced to about forty-eight all ranks. In February 1942 the battalion, once more three companies strong, was incorporated into the 104 Regiment as its third battalion. At the start of Rommel's assault on the Gazala line in May 1942, under the leadership of Hauptmann (Captain) Reissmann, they had taken the important strongpoint of Got el Ualeb. Lt Ringler went to the 10th Company. He was of an old Austrian military family and had a burning ambition to prove himself. As I have explained he kept a diary throughout his service in North Africa and in this first extract describes his journey to join his battalion:

'We are all twenty one years old and crazy. Crazy because we have volunteered of our own free will to go to Africa and have talked about nothing else for weeks and haven't been able to think about anything else either. Fantasy has had free rein—Africa—that's tropical nights, palm trees, sea breezes, natives, oases and tropical helmets. Also a little war, but how can we be anything but victorious? Rommel had taken Tobruk a few days previously, so how long would it be before we were in Cairo, Alexandria and at the Suez Canal? Cairo, and we would be in white tropical uniforms. Previously the **doings of the Afrika Korps had been featured** in the newspapers—by God how we would enjoy that! Out in Africa we wouldn't be one of the crowd and would make a name for ourselves. Day and night we built castles in the air, only to get away from here, away from this morass, a meandering army and the training of recruits. Most of us had already "enjoyed" Russia and had no desire to return to the dirt, the cold and Ivan. But apart from us six optimists, no one in the barracks thought that our application to serve in Africa would come off.

20.7.42
Like madmen we jumped around and hugged each other, we really were going to Africa! In the evening we sat for a long, long time together and couldn't really believe it.

21.7.42
The battalion doctor examined us for tropical fitness. One dropped out because of a slight weakness of the heart. We pitied him. All at once we became a separate caste in the barracks—"The Africans". Our young comrades envied us, the old ones were amused by our enthusiasm—that didn't bother us. Our heaven was full of violins and in Africa there awaited the great adventure. How lucky I was to be getting out of this grey barrack block in which the Emperor's recruits had languished. At twenty one I hadn't really yet found myself—so what had I to lose? Youth, idealism, battle, victory are such intoxicating words. There was nobody there who could offer us better ones.

Top left: 8 MG Battalion loading at Naples, 24 February 1941, on to the German freighters *Wachtfels, Arcturus* and *Alicante.* To reduce possible overall losses during the crossing only a proportion of each company was loaded onto the same ship. The soldiers still wear their field grey uniform./*H. D. Aberger*

Far left, bottom: A 2cm Flak 38 light anti-aircraft gun provides protection to this transport ship during loading./*Col T. Bock*

Bottom left: For the last time this tank has had European soil under its tracks, as the crane lifts it on board a transport ship in Naples harbour./*Col T. Bock*

Bottom centre: Looking down into a ship's hold full of crates containing munitions and food for the DAK./*Col T. Bock*

Below: Goodbye! A crowd of German soldiers wave goodbye to their comrades on a troopship bound for Tripoli./*Col T. Bock*

29

25.7.42

Landau in the Palatinate. It is truly and irrevocably serious. We have seen it in black and white: "transferred to the general orders of the German Afrika Korps". The Regimental Commander has said goodbye to us with mixed feelings. At the station a last clasp of the hand, on the corner could be seen a flowery silk dress and a handkerchief. We are burning our bridges. In Landau we received with reverence the cap of the African reinforcements. The hours went slowly, the waiting was torture.

27.7.42

We drew our tropical clothing. I could hardly believe what wonderful things German soldiers got for war. I received as my most important bit of furniture a huge rubber sealed tropical chest. The contents were really precious—a tropical helmet, a tent, a mosquito net with carrying case, a face veil, a sleeping bag, a pair of desert boots, a pair of tropical shoes, long trousers, short trousers, breeches, coat, blouse, string vests, a body belt of lambs wool—here a little shake of the head—goggles and much, much more. Nobody thought about what would happen to these wonderful things in the future, to which were added a wonderful rucksack, blankets and the usual officers' accoutrements like binoculars, map case, pistol and ammunition pouch etc. There are obviously no sharpshooters in Africa as we hadn't been given a steel helmet. Therefore we thought that the red lined caps must be able to give us great protection.

30.7.42

Munich. Events were moving quickly. We were to be sent to Africa via Munich. Before going we had three days leave. Lt Grabeit swore for the first time at his tropical chest —he was the smallest of us. I didn't feel comfortable at home. The commonplace bits of advice sounded silly: "Don't over-eat on dates and coconuts—Gosh, I'd really like to go with you—This equipment is simply fantastic—You'll get enough shade under the palms—Do you know I really envy you your rations—Did you see on the newsreel how our lads are frying eggs on the sides of their tanks?". I ran away from this rubbish and felt ill at ease.

3.8.42

Journey over the Brenner Pass. We went over the Brenner Pass in pouring rain during a pitch black night. Tired but satisfied we lay on the hard benches and let ourselves be lulled to sleep by the monotonous noise of the wheels, dreaming about Africa which had almost taken form in our minds after all the talking, pictures and ideas.

30

Left: An MG 34 on an anti-aircraft mounting provides protection whilst the ships are loaded. The MG 34 had a 50 round belt linked to form 250 rounds./*Col T. Bock*

Below left: Conditions on board were crowded but everyone could always find a place to eat if they felt like it!/*Bundesarchiv, Koblenz*

Right: A group of Luftwaffe reinforcements sunbathe, eat and play chess on board their troopship./*Col T. Bock*

Below: Another crowded troopship ploughs through choppy seas./*Keystone Press Agency*

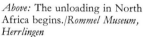
Above: The unloading in North Africa begins./*Rommel Museum, Herrlingen*

Above right: Having reached its destination safely the convoy starts to unload in Tripoli docks. / *Col T. Bock*

4.8.42

Rome. Overawed, we went through this cosmopolitan city with its traffic and pulsating life. The streets were crowded with uniformed, able-bodied Italians. Because they didn't choose to answer our greetings we soon passed them indifferently. We weren't used to the wide variety of goods in the shop windows. We found lodgings in the Albergo di Napoli. A whole day in Rome lay before us as we would not leave until the following evening. The sultry night prevented me from sleeping, bathed in sweat, I tossed from side to side. The hot house heat pressed me almost to the ground, even in the early morning hours. On all sides guides offered to show us the "Eternal City", but we decided to explore on our own. In brutal heat I looked for the Eternal City but in the few hours I had I didn't find it. The Cathedral of St Peter's received me with its overpowering size and refreshing coolness. What a small man I am, struck dumb and moved I left it. Under shadowy arcades I sat with a wonderful ice-cream and then left standing almost a whole glass of fruit juice—a glass of liquid gold. Two years of war seemed to have passed Rome by without a scar. We left for Brindisi in an Italian civilian train. The noise in the station when we left was indescribable. The crowds yelled, shrieked, whistled, screamed and roared. I thought I had entered a mad house. Elegant Italian men and women got into the train by diving through windows, fighting, pulling hair and punching their way to the doors and onto the roofs. We were very happy to have loaded our luggage and

to let ourselves fall peacefully into the red upholstered seats. Our uniforms stuck to our bodies, each movement started us sweating. An unbearable itch on my neck woke me from my half sleep. Bugs, thousands of bugs! We fled into the passageway. Outside a dreary landscape went past. The farther south we got the flatter and drier the land became. Vineyards, olive groves, rocks, the sun standing overhead, and tattered, slovenly men. A few cacti and palms reminded us of the journey's end. I had the feeling that even we would soon become tired and indifferent in these surroundings. What would it be like in Africa?

6.8.42

Brindisi. The first impressions were depressing. Nothing for our imaginations to catch hold of. Family life was played out on the streets. Naked, dirty children ran between my feet. Dirty alleyways, bombed houses and primitive ruins, seedy Italian marines were everywhere in the town, drunk and shouting as they swarmed over the whole area. Near the harbour we bathed in the sea. The oily layer on the water disgusted me almost as much as the greasy smell of macaroni. The camp was in a foul, bombed ruin. In the middle of the room was a naked, dazzling electric bulb—in spite of the bugs and noise from all corners of the town, we slept. Nice and early in a rainy darkness we flew off from the aerodrome. I was in a Junkers JU52 with fifteen men, nine of whom were officers, with all our weapons and luggage stowed away. I flew for the first time. It felt odd to begin

Left: An SdKfz 251/7 half tracked personnel carrier is unloaded. It carried a crew of two plus nine passengers./*Brig P. A. L. Vaux*

Below: An 8.8cm Flak 18—the scourge of Allied armour and best known of all anti-tank weapons—is lowered ashore.
Brig P. A. L. Vaux

Above: A group of disembarking soldiers pose in front of their SdKfz 251/7 half track./*Brig P. A. L. Vaux*

with, the sight of the world from above was unique. The people were little dots, the ships in the harbour like toys, then the endless sea. The monotonous noise of the motors and the heat and tiredness made me fall asleep. When I woke again I saw the Greek islands somewhat covered by haze, still indescribably beautiful. As the water became shallower by the shore the islands were surrounded by the whole spectrum of colours from deep blue to bright green. The aeroplanes banked over towards the landing field at Maleme in Crete. Under us there were piles of destroyed JU52s, signs of the hard battles that had raged there a year ago.'

Lt Ringler spent a few hours in Crete and then flew on to Africa. Here is how he described his final landfall on this eventful journey:

'We flew low over the British controlled Mediterranean Sea. Bashfully Gunter asked if there were any life jackets. The pilot only grinned. They were totally useless. We were flying so low so that Tommy wouldn't see us that, if in spite of this he did, then any attempt to escape would be impossible. We couldn't climb and if we were shot down we would plunge into the water within seconds. Nobody would be able to get out of the machine so why bother with life jackets? He

was right. "But we've got a machine gun", I interjected. The pilot laughed again, "totally full of sand and roasted, not one shot will come from that again". This was my first taste of the attitude of "Kismet" of those who fought in Africa. The dark green sea with its white crests, the regular buzzing of the engines and the heat finally made me fall asleep. I awoke confused, the sun seemed even more dazzling, the heat more powerful. My uniform clung to my body. Then I saw a flash out of the sun and started —an enemy hunter! The pilot had seen him a long time ago and was amused at our fear. "German fighter cover from Tobruk".

"Haven't we had any fighter protection all the way from Crete?"

"No, Lieutenant, we've been lucky. Yesterday a formation of forty-six JUs was shot down completely".

Whilst I once more pondered the meaning of the arab Kismet, the pilot dug me in the ribs and pointed below. We had climbed higher and I could see the sea below us and, as if drawn by a ruler, the African coast, and the dazzling orange yellow plain—the desert. "Tobruk!" That was a couple of white spots around a bay. My eyes were blinded by the glare when the JU52 jolted to a halt. Suddenly the pilots became very hurried.

"Quickly out, come on hurry, we don't want

Above: German troops boarding
a Junkers JU52 en route for
North Africa, February 1942.
IWM

Left: A Junkers JU52 being
loaded with supplies and soldiers
for North Africa, January 1942.
/IWM

to be caught with our trousers down in the desert. Hurry!"

We could only just throw out out kit and then the corrugated iron bird rolled off. Africa and the desert received us with sun, heat and a wind that threw the sand into our faces in handfuls. In an instant one's eyes gummed up. We didn't know whether to ask or to order the soldiers to carry our officers' chests. They formed up and marched off. Where should we go now?

"Posted to the DAK"—that's what is said in our marching orders. We tried to orientate ourselves. On the huge airfield planes took off and landed constantly, so we had to get away from there as quickly as possible. To the north we saw dust clouds a long way away—perhaps a road. Swearing and sweating, we dragged ourselves and our chests with their "equipment necessary for Africa" towards it. Mosquito nets, small and large, sheets, underwear, body belts, shirts, socks, boots and so on. On our heads we wore the most important item—the tropical helmet. *Heia Safari!"*

First Taste of the Desert
On arrival some reinforcements seemed to be treated much as one might expect, remembering the shortages under which the DAK had to operate, and reached their units quickly. Karl Schwiedergall, however, who was a gunner in an anti aircraft battery had this cautionary tale to tell:

Far left: A JU52 crossing the North African coast loaded with supplies for the Afrika Korps. /*Bundesarchiv, Koblenz*

Left: A JU52 (called affectionately *Tante JU* (Auntie JU)) brings petrol to the vehicles of 8 MG Bn who had run out of fuel at Ben Gania airport./*H. D. Aberger*

Below: Soldiers, plus their personal kit, waiting to board a Junkers JU52 for North Africa. / *Bundesarchiv, Koblenz*

'In the Afrika Korps I was a gunner in an anti aircraft 8.8 battery, which was employed in the ground battle against tanks. The number of my battery was 1 Battery Flak Regiment I/43. The first parts of my Regiment were flown across from Italy in November 1941 to Tripoli. I arrived in February 1942 in Tripoli by air from Trapani. Funnily enough my battery was at the time of my arrival far away from Tripoli. All reinforcements had to stay in a barracks outside the town, which was called "Kilometer 5". The Commandant of the barracks was a bully type chap, known throughout the Afrika Korps. He tried to keep troops as long as possible for fatigue and guard duties. The second battery of my Regiment heard that reinforcements had arrived and tried to get me with others out of "Kilometer 5". The Commandant refused, so they broke the lock of the rear entrance and out we went along the Via Balbia to my own battery which I found to be in Benghazi'.

Karl Susenberger's arrival at his unit was perhaps more typical:
'After landing at Derna we were taken at once to a collecting centre, here we were registered and earmarked for different divisions. A few friends and I were selected for 21 Panzer Division, those that remained of my comrades went to 15 Panzer or 90 Light. We had some time before the vehicles came; I went up a hill with a few buddies and saw

the endlessly wide desert in front of us. Towards evening the vehicles of 21 Panzer Division came to collect us. We were showered with dust and dirt for the whole journey and could only see if we wore goggles. When we arrived we brushed as much dirt off us as possible. After ten minutes we had to fall in and a captain said to us "You've had your first look at Africa—it will get worse I promise you".

We were then divided amongst the various regiments. With Günther Halm, Otte, Dannheim and a few others, I was allocated to 104 Schützen-Regiment (Motorised Infantry). Finally we were taken to the regiment. Meanwhile it had got dark and when we arrived evening rations were distributed and then we went to sleep. Rations consisted of tubes of processed cheese, sardines in oil, some bread and lemon juice, in the next few weeks we realised that these were standard Afrika Korps rations.

The next morning Lieutenant Müller greeted us and asked about our training. Afterwards we were split up—the anti-tank gunners to the Heavy company, we radio operators stayed with the Regimental Headquarters.

Lt Müller said, "You will stay here for the next few days until you are sent to your battalions".

We were again tested over the next few days for they wanted to get a good idea of our proficiency. Three days later Lt Müller told us, "Susenburger and Dannheim have been detailed for the 3rd Battalion. You will be fetched later today".

That afternoon a motorbike and sidecar came to collect us. We reported to the sergeant major in the orderly room tent where we were somewhat critically inspected. After giving our particulars Sergeant Major Golz received us. He said "You'll be all right here, they're all first-rate lads".

They were indeed and we soon got on with them. After a few hours we had to report to Lt Kordel. He welcomed us and wished us well with the battalion, but acclimatisation was difficult. I got dysentry and was on the bog all day. Trousers were more often down than up, but it passed and in a few days everything was OK. One evening when the food was being handed out there was suddenly a shout, "Achtung!" and the cook NCO saluted a major and reported to him. When he had gone I learnt that he was our battalion commander Major Ehle. In the next few days I also learnt that our battalion had been recently formed from the former Motor Cycle Battalion 15 and was now called the Third Battalion, Regiment 104.

My birthday, the 12 May neared, I was 19. As I shaved Sergeant Major Golz came to congratulate me. It had got round very quickly and was a hilarious and convivial affair—and at 50 degrees C. (122F)! The next morning I had to report to the sergeant major in the orderly room. Off I went,

Top left: As the first detachments of the DAK arrive on North African soil, the German National Anthem is played by a small welcoming band./*Col T. Bock*

Centre left: German troops marching through Tripoli on 27 February 1941./*Col T. Bock*

Bottom left: An immaculate tank commander in the turret of his panzer as the parade passes a statue of Mussolini under the palms of Tripoli./*Col T. Bock*

Above: Rommel reviewing his newly arrived troops—Note his Corps Commander's pennant (a black triangle over a red triangle on a white background, with the word *AFRIKA* on the red field)./*Col T. Bock*

Above: Rommel, accompanied by General Garibaldi, greeting Italian officers during the arrival parade, 27 February 1941. / *Bundesarchiv, Koblenz*

Right: Rommel, riding in a staff car with General Garibaldi, Italian C in C in North Africa during the inspection on 27 February 1941. / *Bundesarchiv, Koblenz*

Left: Get your knees brown! The first inspection in shorts can be a little embarrassing!/*Col T. Bock*

Below left: The crew of Panzer 801 obligingly giving a native boy a lift in the desert./*Col T. Bock*

noticing a low-flying ME109 about 500 metres away and coming closer. The pilot must have seen me for he "buzzed" me, indeed he was so low that I had to fling myself onto the ground. He repeated this manoeuvre twice before buzzing off in a sharp curve. Everyone had seen this and the sergeant major said "He must have been pissed".

In the following days we practised on the radio with the occasional lesson, so that afterwards in action everything would be perfect. One day we were playing dice, only for amusement, when Grimm had the following idea: "Whoever loses will have to shave his skull".

We thought for a while and then agreed. In the end it became obvious who had to have their hair cut—Bernd Rey, Grimm, Hossfeld and I. Immediately we went to work. The denuded heads were shaved really smooth, so that they shone beautifully. Everyone was proud of his bald pate and because we wore our forage caps during the day nothing could be seen of them. Even our superiors didn't realise at first, but after it had got round we were nicknamed "The Baldies". OK so from then on we were the baldies. We had to take a lot of ribbing from our mates, but it was all in fun. The rumour went round that we'd have to go into action fairly soon. A few days later it was confirmed, but before this the battalion attended a field service. It was on the 24th May that the battalion fell in in horseshoe order for divine service. Next to the priest stood Major Ehle, on the left stood the battalion staff officers, in the middle and on the right stood 9 and 11 Companies respectively, and as it just so happened, we four bald men stood next to each other in the first rank. When it started and everyone had to take their caps off for prayers, our bald pates shone so beautifully that a light giggling began amongst the officers of the companies. Major Ehle looked at us darkly and we knew only too well what that meant. The telling off came from Lt Kordel, hardly had we been fallen out than we had to report to him. We let this telling off wash over us because we had thick skins and with that the matter was dropped. Lt Kordel was really a good chap, above all not one to bear a grudge'.

41

Organisation and Tactics

What's in a name?

It is interesting to see that, just in the same way as the title 'The Desert Rats', which strictly speaking should only be applied to the men of the British Seventh Armoured Division, has become the generally accepted name for all the British troops who fought in the Desert, so the title 'The Afrika Korps' is used to describe all those German troops who opposed them. In actual fact the Afrika Korps was only a small part of Rommel's command which was officially known by various titles during the period 1941-1943.

Deutsches Afrika Korps

On 19 February 1941 a directive from Adolf Hitler's headquarters announced that the German forces in North Africa, under the command of Generalleutnant Erwin Rommel, would henceforth be called the *Deutsches Afrika Korps (DAK)*. About a week before this announcement Rommel had established a small headquarters staff (*Aufklärungstab Rommel*) in Africa which was automatically absorbed into his new command.

On its formation the DAK consisted basically of two Divisions—5th Light (5 leichte) and 15 Panzer. *5 leichte Division* was the original blocking force sent out to prevent further advances westwards by the British. It was made up mainly of men and equipment from 3 Panzer Division and many of its vehicles carried the 3 Panzer symbol (see drawings). The leading elements of the division, which consisted of its reconnaissance and anti-tank battalions, arrived in Tripoli on 14 February 1941. Its armour (Panzer Regiment 5) followed a few days later. 5 leichte was reorganised, strengthened and retitled *21 Panzer Division* on 1 October 1941. When it landed Panzer Regiment 5 had approximately 120 tanks, only half of which were Pzkw IIIs and IVs. *15 Panzer Division*'s leading elements arrived in Africa in late April 1942. By mid June it was complete and shortly afterwards was heavily engaged against British armour in the 'Battle-axe' offensive. Both divisions remained in Africa throughout the campaign, surrendering to the Allied forces in May 1943.

Panzergruppe Afrika

On 15 August 1941 Rommel's command was raised to the status of a Panzergruppe. By this time the DAK had been joined by *90 leichte Division* which was initially formed in August 1941 as the 'Afrika Division'. It consisted of various independent units which were already serving in Africa, plus troops ferried across the Mediterranean by air. The Division's first major action was the assault on Tobruk on 21 November 1941. Later that month it was given the title: *90 leichte*. In addition, six Italian divisions—the Ariete, Trieste, Pavia, Bologna, Bresica and Savonia —were also put under Rommel's command. Panzergruppe Headquarters was at Beda Littoria. By the end of January 1942 the title had changed to *Panzerarmee Afrika* and it was also known as the *deutsche—italienische*

Part of a recce battalion, including two Sd Kfz 222 light armoured cars formed up for a ceremony—possibly the presentation of decorations.
/*Bundesarchiv, Koblenz*

Panzerarmee. About a year later this title was discontinued in favour of *1 italienische Armee*.

Stab Nehring/XC Korps

General der Panzertruppe Walther Nehring, returned to Africa in November 1942—he had been evacuated after being wounded in the arm on 31 August 1942 whilst commanding the DAK—and assumed command of all German forces in Tunisia. The title was shortly afterwards changed to XC Korps.

Panzer-Armee Ober kommando (5 Pz AOK 5)

Formed early in December 1942 in order to strengthen the command structure in Tunisia, it absorbed XC Korps. General Nehring was its first commander, followed in March 1943 by Generaloberst Jürgen von Arnim.

Heeresgruppe—Afrika

After the deutsche—italienische Panzerarmee arrived in Tunisia the forces involved there were considered too strong for proper control by one Army Headquarters. So a *Heeresgruppe* (*Army Group*) was formed under Rommel, who had been promoted to the rank of Generalfeldmarschall on 22 July 1942 after finally capturing Tobruk. The Heeresgruppe consisted of the deutsche-italienische Panzerarmee now under command of the Italian General di Armata Messe, and PzAOK 5 under Generaloberst von Arnim. Rommel

was destined to leave Africa before the final collapse and it was left to von Arnim, as his successor, to surrender on behalf of the staffs of the Heeresgruppe and the DAK at noon on 12 May 1943.

Symbols

Afrika Korps

Most famous symbol of all, the palm and swastika was carried on most vehicles including tanks, lorries, recce vehicles etc, belonging to 15 and 21 Panzer Divisions which made up the bulk of the Afrika Korps. It was generally in white.

Balkenkreuz

The Balkenkreuz appeared on almost every German vehicle in North Africa, for example, on the sides of the hull and/or rear hull plate of all tanks.

Divisional Symbols

(Mainly in white or black, sometimes in yellow)

5 leichte

This was the original 'blocking force' which was sent out in February 1941 to bolster up the Italians and prevent further advance westwards by the British. This symbol did not appear on 5 leichte vehicles.

3 Panzer

3 Panzer Division supplied men, vehicles and equipment to form 5 leichte Division.

Top right: Signpost of HQ 21 Panzer Division, 6km south of Chechiban and 44km west of A. el Gazala, 21 May 1942. /*Bundesarchiv, Koblenz*

Bottom right: The Nazi flag provides a very clear ground to air recognition symbol on this Volkswagen (C PKW K1). The pennant appears to be that of a divisional commander. /*Bundesarchiv, Koblenz*

Below: The Afrika Korps symbol is very clearly seen on the side of this Kfz 81 light AA vehicle, equipped here with a 20mm Flak 38 dual purpose gun, being used in its anti-tank role. /*Bundesarchiv, Koblenz*

This symbol was therefore to be found on some AFVs and other vehicles of 5 leichte.

21 Panzer
On 1 October 1941, 5 leichte Division was reorganised, strengthened and retitled '21 Panzer Division'. It continued to fight throughout the remainder of the campaign in North Africa.

15 Panzer
The other original division of the Afrika Korps was 15 Panzer which arrived in Africa during April—June 1941. It also fought with distinction throughout the North African campaign.

90 leichte
Initially organised as the 'Afrika Division' it was redesignated 90 leichte on 27 November 1941. It took part in most major battles throughout the campaign.

10 Panzer
Assigned to XC Corps in Tunisia in November 1942. It fought there until the battered remnants surrendered on 9 May 1943.

164 leichte Afrika
Flown to Africa in July 1942 the symbol of crossed swords over the continent of Africa was not introduced until December 1942.

Afrika Korps

Balkenkreuz

DIVISIONAL SYMBOLS

Ramcke Parachute Brigade

5   leichte

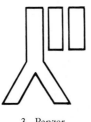

3   Panzer

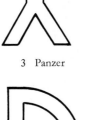

or

21   Panzer

INSIGNIA

Tropical Breast Eagle

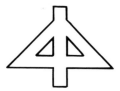

15   Panzer

90   leichte

Tropical Helmet Shields

Left

Right

10   Panzer

164   leichte Afrika

CUFF TITLE

334   Infanterie

999   leichte Afrika

334 Infanterie

Arrived in Africa in November 1942 and was continually engaged in Tunisia until 8 May 1943 when the Division plus some smaller units surrendered to the British.

999 leichte Afrika

Formed originally as a Brigade which consisted mainly of court martialled German soldiers to whom combat duty had been authorised for purposes of rehabilitation. It was redesignated 999 leichte Afrika—Division in March 1943.

Ramcke Parachute Brigade

Arrived late summer in 1942 when the Germans were pinned down in front of El Alamein as Rommel's only reinforcements apart from 164 leichte. Fought magnificently throughout the withdrawal. The small letter in the lower right corner indicated the battalion and its commander (eg H—Hübner)

Insignia

Tropical Breast Eagle

Although this was of standard design, the eagle was in light blue embroidery on a copper-brown base. It was worn above the right breast pocket on the tropical field blouse.

Tropical Helmet Shields

Two lightweight metal shields were attached to the sides of the tropical or pith helmet. On the left side was a dull silver wehrmacht eagle on a black background, on the right the national colours—black/white/red.

Above: The Afrika Korps cuff title was awarded after two month's service in Africa. It was later replaced by the *Afrika* cuff title which had the status of a campaign decoration./*IWM*

Left: A group of Panzer Grenadiers from 15 Pz Div. The Obergefreiter (Corporal) is wearing the infantry assault badge on his left breast pocket and the ribbon of his Iron Cross 2nd class in the usual button hole./*IWM*

47

Cuff Titles 'Afrika Korps' and 'Afrika'

Cuff titles were worn in the German Army for three reasons:

(a) Those awarded as a battle honour and were thus the equivalent of a campaign medal.

(b) Those worn by certain elite army units and formations.

(c) Those worn by personnel of a training school, command staff or special formation.

There were two such cuff titles in DAK:

(a) *Afrika Korps*—Instituted 18 July 1941, authorised for wear by all members of DAK fighting in North Africa. 3.3cm wide with silver block lettering on a dark green background. It was then edged top and bottom with a band of silver .3cm wide. This title was worn on the right cuff of service, field service and uniform tunics as well as the great coat. A minimum of two month's service in Africa was required before an individual was permitted to wear the Afrika Korps cuff title.

(b) *Afrika*. On 13 January 1943 the Führer ordered the introduction of an Afrika cuff title which had the status of a campaign decoration and was the same for all three branches of the Wehrmacht. It was of similar size and construction to the Afrika Korps cuff title but had two palm trees flanking the inscription 'Afrika'. The following conditions were set up by the OKW for the awarding of this cuff title:

(1) At least six months' service on African soil.

(2) Being wounded in combat in the North African theatre.

(3) The contraction of an illness whilst in the North African theatre of war which demanded evacuation to the continent. At least three months' service required before contracting the illness.

Any of the above requirements were considered fulfilled if an individual was killed on duty in North Africa. In this case only the award document was presented to his dependents. No foreigner was eligible for the 'Afrika' cuff title.

Panzer Divisions

The main strength of the Afrika Korps lay without doubt in its Panzer Divisions, so it is as well to understand their basic organisation. It is however, very difficult to generalise as far as the DAK was concerned because each of its formations evolved over a period of time and none remained constant for very long. However, if one takes 15 Panzer and 21 Panzer Divisions as examples and looks at their basic organisation about mid-1942, then this gives a reasonable impression of

Comparison of British/German armour and anti-armour capabilities.

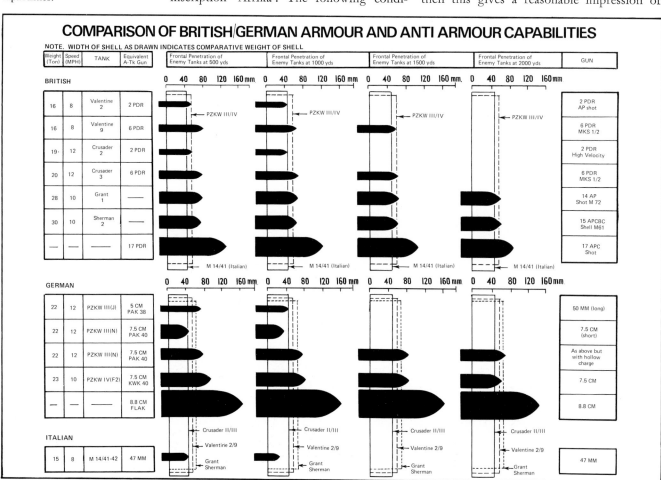

COMPARISON OF BRITISH/GERMAN ARMOUR AND ANTI ARMOUR CAPABILITIES

NOTE. WIDTH OF SHELL AS DRAWN INDICATES COMPARATIVE WEIGHT OF SHELL

Weight (Ton)	Speed (MPH)	TANK	Equivalent A-Tk Gun	Frontal Penetration of Enemy Tanks at 500 yds	Frontal Penetration of Enemy Tanks at 1000 yds	Frontal Penetration of Enemy Tanks at 1500 yds	Frontal Penetration of Enemy Tanks at 2000 yds	GUN
BRITISH								
16	8	Valentine 2	2 PDR					2 PDR AP shot
16	8	Valentine 9	6 PDR					6 PDR MKS 1/2
19·	12	Crusader 2	2 PDR					2 PDR High Velocity
20	12	Crusader 3	6 PDR					6 PDR MKS 1/2
28	10	Grant 1	—					14 AP Shot M 72
30	10	Sherman 2	—					15 APCBC Shell M61
—	—	—	17 PDR					17 APC Shot
GERMAN								
22	12	PZKW III(J)	5 CM PAK 38					50 MM (long)
22	12	PZKW III(N)	7.5 CM PAK 40					7.5 CM (short)
22	12	PZKW III(N)	7.5 CM PAK 40					As above but with hollow charge
23	10	PZKW IV(F2)	7.5 CM KWK 40					7.5 CM
—	—	—	8.8 CM FLAK					8.8 CM
ITALIAN								
15	8	M 14/41-42	47 MM					47 MM

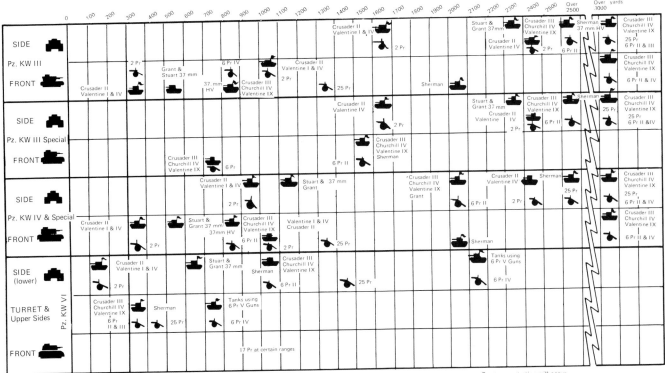

NOTES:—

For the purpose of this diagram it is assumed.
1. That the amn. used is as follows:—

37.00 mm	M61AP
2 Pr A.P.	CBC
6 Pr II & III A.P. (L.V.)	APCBC(HV)
6 Pr IV & V —	APCBC (HV)
75.00 mm	
Sherman —	M61APCBC
25 Pr A.P.	APC (Supercharge)

2. That all strikes are at 30° to normal

3. That the shot strikes the average thickness or armour at front or side

4. The front armour of all German tanks (except Mk VI) is face-hardened, the front armour of Mk III Special is spaced.

Greater penetration will occur
1. At normal impact
2. If the shot strikes a joint or place where the armour is thinner than average

Lesser penetration will occur
1. At angles over 30° to normal
2. If the shell strikes a place where the armour is thicker than average
3. If the wrong amn. is used.

Above: The British gun v The German tank.

Left: The German gun v The British tank.

NOTES:—

For the purpose of this diagram it is assumed:
1. That the amn. used is APHE or APCBCHE shell.
2. That the shell strikes at 30° to normal.
3. That it strikes the average thickness of armour at front or side

GREATER penetration will occur:
1. At normal impact.
2. If the shell strikes a joint or a place where the armour is thinner than average
3. With 'arrowhead' amn. up to 500 yds range

LESSER penetration will occur:
1. At angles over 30° to normal
2. If the shell penetrates a place where the armour is thicker than average

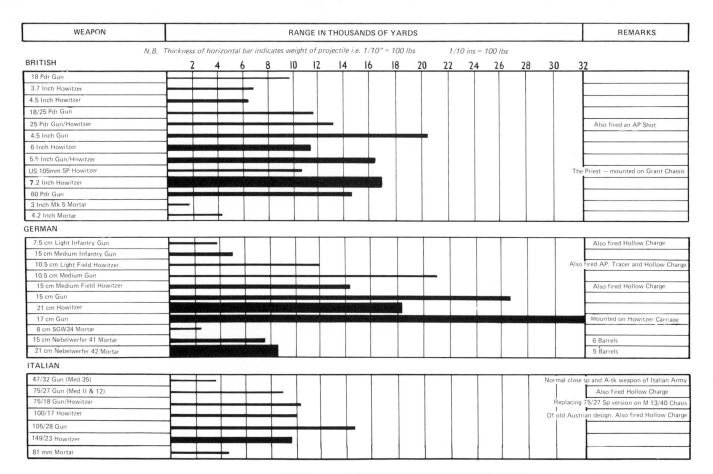

WEAPON	RANGE IN THOUSANDS OF YARDS	REMARKS
N.B. Thickness of horizontal bar indicates weight of projectile i.e. 1/10" = 100 lbs	1/10 ins = 100 lbs	
BRITISH	2 4 6 8 10 12 14 16 18 20 22 24 26 28 30 32	
18 Pdr Gun		
3.7 Inch Howitzer		
4.5 Inch Howitzer		
18/25 Pdr Gun		
25 Pdr Gun/Howitzer		Also fired an AP Shot
4.5 Inch Gun		
6 Inch Howitzer		
5.5 Inch Gun/Howitzer		
US 105mm SP Howitzer		The Priest — mounted on Grant Chassis
7.2 Inch Howitzer		
60 Pdr Gun		
3 Inch Mk 5 Mortar		
4.2 Inch Mortar		
GERMAN		
7.5 cm Light Infantry Gun		Also fired Hollow Charge
15 cm Medium Infantry Gun		
10.5 cm Light Field Howitzer		Also fired AP. Tracer and Hollow Charge
10.5 cm Medium Gun		
15 cm Medium Field Howitzer		Also fired Hollow Charge
15 cm Gun		
21 cm Howitzer		
17 cm Gun		Mounted on Howitzer Carriage
8 cm 5GW34 Mortar		
15 cm Nebelwerfer 41 Mortar		6 Barrels
21 cm Nebelwerfer 42 Mortar		5 Barrels
ITALIAN		
47/32 Gun (Med 35)		Normal close sp and A-tk weapon of Italian Army
75/27 Gun (Med II & 12)		Also fired Hollow Charge
75/18 Gun/Howitzer		Replacing 75/27 Sp version on M 13/40 Chasis
100/17 Howitzer		Of old Austrian design. Also fired Hollow Charge
105/28 Gun		
149/23 Howitzer		
81 mm Mortar		

the types of units within such a division. These were:

Divisional Headquarters
Reconnaissance Unit
Signals Battalion
Tank Regiment
Lorried Infantry Brigade
Artillery Regiment
Anti-Tank Battalion
Anti-Aircraft Battalion
Engineer Battalion
Medical Unit
Services (eg Supply, Administrative, Provost and Postal Units).
Note: This organisation has been taken from the AFV Field Pocket Book 1942 as issued by the War Office.

In the following pages I have tried to give a comprehensive idea of the various unit organisations and to show in pictures some of their weapons, Armoured Fighting Vehicles (AFV) and equipment.

The Mechanised Reconnaissance Unit (Aufklärungs—Abteilung (mot))
This was a battalion-sized unit (AA3 in 21 Pz Div and AA33 in 15 Pz Div) with the task of obtaining information rapidly, for example in confirmation of air reconnaissance or where a clear picture of the enemy's situation could only be gained by fighting.

Top left: Comparison of British/German artillery capabilities.

Centre left: Which way to Cairo? A recce motorcyclist checking up on his route!/*Bundesarchiv, Koblenz*

Bottom left: A light armoured car Sd Kfz 222 negotiating rocky terrain. This excellent AFV was armed with a 20mm cannon and a 7.92mm machine gun./*IWM*

Right: Close-up of the turret of a Sd Kfz 222 showing the 20mm cannon. It had a crew of three and a top speed of 50mph./*IWM*

Below: The Sd Kfz 231 heavy armoured car, which had drive and steering to all eight wheels. This version mounted a 7.5cm tank gun (formerly mounted in the Pz Kw IV)./*IWM*

Bottom: This version of the Sd Kfz 231 heavy armoured car mounted a 20mm cannon and a 7.92mm machine gun. (The donkey is unarmed!) /*Keystone Press Agency Ltd*

It was specially equipped for this task with armoured cars and a large number of automatic weapons. The unit moved fast and had the ability to operate over a wide radius of action—up to 60 miles in width and up to 60 miles ahead of the division. It consisted of:

(a) Two armoured car companies—each with an HQ of 4 light (lt) armoured cars (Armd cs); one heavy (hy) armd c platoon (pl) of 6 hy armd cs (eg Sd Kfz 231); two lt armd c pls each of 6 lt armd cs (eg Sd Kfz 222).

(b) One of more fully mechanised rifle companies—each with an HQ; three pls of 3 sections (sect) each (2 x LMG per sect) and a lt mortar sect (1 x 5cm mor); a machine gun pl with 2 machine guns on heavy mountings. All sections travelled in half tracks (eg Sd Kfz 251).

(c) A heavy company comprising—a close support pl of 2 x 75mm self-propelled guns; an anti-tank pl of 3 x 37mm anti tank guns; an engineer pl, with the capability of building a 5 ton 35ft bridge or 2 x 2 ton rafts or one 4 ton raft (not often used in the Western Desert!)

Depending upon the task, battle groups (*Kampfgruppe*) would be formed comprising all elements of the unit operating as all arms teams. As explained the unit often worked

51

Left: An Sd Kfz 251 recce half track belonging to 21 Pz Div outside the German base at Tmimi, March 1942. /*H. D. Aberger*

Below: An Sd Kfz 251 recce half track which had a range of 185 miles and a speed of 31mph, is seen here outside a desert fort in Cyrenaica./*Associated Press*

Top right: A signalman testing a land line./*Col T. Bock*

Bottom right: Cross country line laying in a Kfz 23 telephone communications car. /*Bundesarchiv, Koblenz*

in conjunction with air recce—a squadron normally being attached to a particular Panzer division. Recce aircraft could make their reports by radio, by message dropping or verbally on landing; but radio was preferred as the observer could then be questioned from the ground and given new tasks.

Signals Battalion (Nachrichten—Abteilung (mot))
Communications are the lifeblood of any fast moving armoured formation and in the desert radios were widely used. Armoured cross country signal trucks accompanied the tanks wherever they went and supplied the communications so necessary to the commanders for the control of their forces. Powerful sets connected all the major units to Divisional Headquarters and because of the speed at which the tanks advanced, large numbers of spare sets were kept for further deployment. Line communications, especially to higher command, were maintained as long as possible and civil telephone lines were used when they were available.

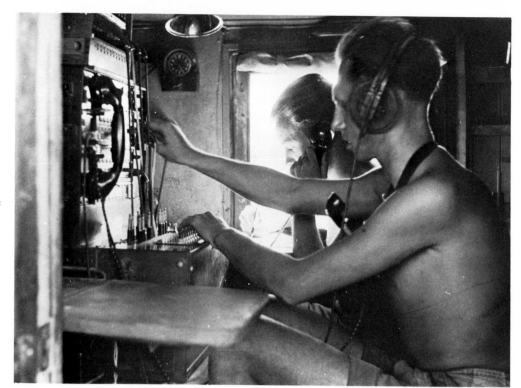

Right: Inside a telephone exchange vehicle of HQ 21 Panzer Div. /*Bundesarchiv, Koblenz*

Below: Erecting an aerial on the rear of a Kfz 17 wireless car at HQ 21 Panzer Division, May 1942./*Bundesarchiv, Koblenz*

Below right: A Signals radio vehicle with a large aerial mast at HQ 21 Panzer Division, May 1942. Note the signalman operating a pedal generator behind the van. /*Bundesarchiv, Koblenz*

Tank Regiment (Panzer Regiment)

The basic organisation of the Tank Regiment had been altered three times between the start of the war and 1942. When the German panzers swept victoriously through Europe, regiments consisted of two battalions, each of four companies. They contained a total of 204 tanks of which 136 were light *Panzer Kampfwagens* (Armoured Combat Vehicles)— normally abbreviated to Pz Kpfw or just Pz Kw—Marks I and II, and only 68 medium and heavy Pz Kws—Marks III and IV. When the DAK arrived in Africa 5 and 8 Panzer Regiments were each organised in two battalions, each of three companies. However, by 1942 they had changed their organisation to three battalions each of three companies. Most Mark Is had been eliminated and the 201 tanks comprised 69 Mark II, 102 Mark III and 30 Mark IV. The battalions were divided into two light tank companies and one medium tank company. The complete breakdown being:

HQ Pz Regt—1 Pz Kw III, 2 hy Armoured Command Vehicles (ACV), 5 Pz Kw II (Protection pl).

Three Battalions—each of 65 tanks—comprising:

(a)   HQ—as for the Pz Regt, plus Engineer pl, Motorcycle pl, Anti Aircraft pl.

(b)   Two light tank companies, with a total of 22 tanks each:
HQ—5 Pz Kw II, 2 Pz Kw III. Three pls each—5 Pz Kw III.

(c)   One medium tank company, with a total of 15 tanks:
HQ—5 Pz Kw II, 2 Pz Kw IV. Two pls each —4 Pz Kw IV.

By 1943 the organisation had changed again and the numbers of tanks in the Panzer battalion reduced to 48—basically three companies each of three platoons of 4 tanks and only 2 tanks in Coy HQs. A small number of Tiger tanks (Panzer Battalion 501) were used in Tunisia towards the end of the North African campaign as well as most Marks of Pz Kws as the photographs on these pages show.

The success of the tank regiment depended

Below: Pz Kw I light tanks on parade. The tank commanders are wearing full parade uniform including the distinctive Panzer Beret (*Schutzmütze*). Note also Hitler, Mussolini and Goering on the saluting base. The 6.4 ton tank only carried two 7.92mm machine guns and was very lightly armoured./*IWM*

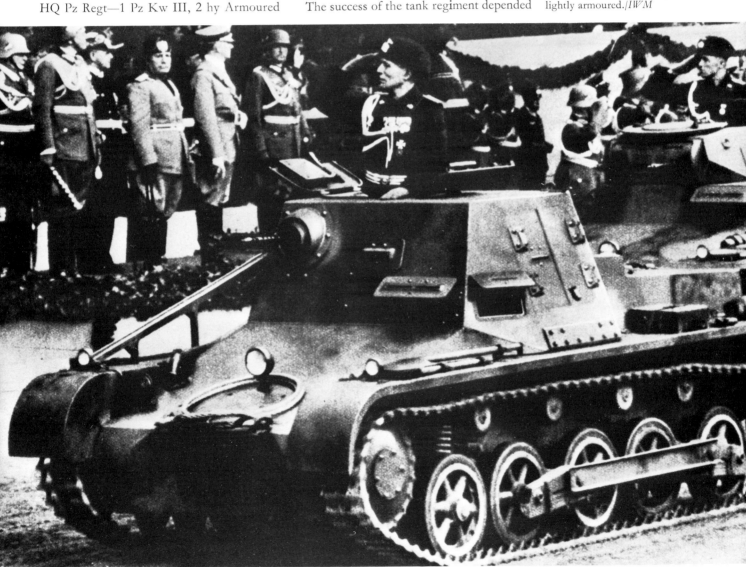

upon its employment en masse and the concentration of a very large number of tanks for a surprise thrust deep into the enemy's weak spots was one of Rommel's favourite manoeuvres. German tanks were undoubtedly able to outrange and outgun British tanks and held their superiority until the arrival on the scene of the American built Shermans and Grants. The charts which accompany this section show their superiority graphically. However, the German tanks were less mechanically reliable, due to the wear and tear caused by sand and dust acting on their inadequately filtered engines. This reduced engine life to about one third of normal and threw an even heavier burden on the repair and supply system.

Above: The Pz Kw II weighed 11.2 tons and was armed with a 20mm gun and a 7.92mm machine gun./*IWM*

Centre left: A tank crewman standing proudly in front of his Pz Kw II light tank (note his small silver death's head collar badges). Only lightly armoured (11.2 tons) it was armed with a 20mm gun and a 7.92mm machine gun./*Brig P. A. L. Vaux*

Bottom left: A Pz Kw III Ausf J/H moving at speed. It was armed with a 5cm gun instead of the original 37mm.
/*Brig P. A. L. Vaux*

Above: A Pz Kw III Ausf F/G with a 5cm gun. It weighed 20 tons, had a crew of 5, a top speed of 25mph and a range of 109 miles./*H. L. Turner*

Centre left: The Pz Kw III Ausf L/M was armed with a longer L/60 5cm gun and two 7.92mm MG 34 machine guns./*Col T. Bock*

Bottom left: Pz Kw III Ausf N. The model N had the short L/24 75mm gun from the Pz Kw IV and was for close support. /*Col T. Bock*

Above: A well laden Pz Kw III. Note the jerricans and ammunition boxes. In the background is an 88mm AA/ATk gun towed by a Sd Kfz 251/7.
/Bundesarchiv, Koblenz

Centre right: A Pz Kw IV (F2) which was armed with the long barrelled L/48 75mm gun was probably the best tank in the Western Desert./*K. Susenberger*

Bottom right: This Pz Kw IV has been camouflaged very effectively to look like a lorry. Both sides used this stratagem to disguise their AFVs./*K. Susenberger*

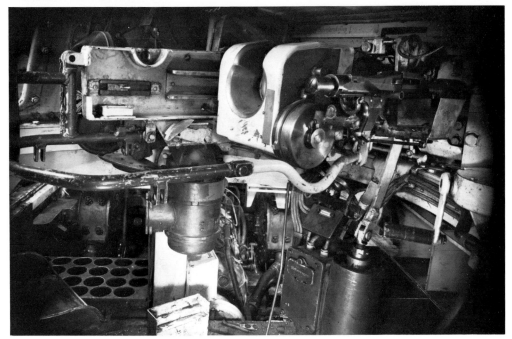

Above: A Pz Kw IV armed with the long barrelled 75mm gun is seen here in a sandbagged emplacement. The high velocity long barrelled gun replaced the short barrelled low velocity 75mm which was rather ineffective against enemy armour.
/Col T. Bock

Centre left: Inside view of a Pz Kw IV turret looking from the loader's side. The gunner's telescope brow pad is just visible behind the 75mm run out shield. The MG 34 coaxially mounted machine gun can be seen on the right of the main gun. Note also the empty ammunition bin on the floor with a swivel seat./*IWM*

Bottom left: This 54 ton Tiger tank was knocked out by 7th Armoured Division just outside Tunis./*Lt Col A. H. Stanton*

Lorried Infantry Brigade (Schützen—Brigade (mot))

In 1942 this consisted of two regiments of motorised infantry (*Panzer Grenadiers*) and a motorcycle battalion (*Kradschützen*). The complete breakdown of the lorried infantry regiment was as follows:

Regimental HQ
HQ Company—Sig pl, Pioneer pl, Motorcycle DR pl.
2 x Battalions each—HQ
3 x Rifle coys each with 220 men and 3 x 5cm mortars, 2 x Hy MGs, 18 x LMGs, MG coy —6 x 81mm mortars and 8 x Hy MGs, Heavy coy—Lt Inf Gun pl—2 x 75mm support guns, ATk pl—3 x 37mm or 50mm ATk guns, Pnr pl.
Inf Gun coy—4 x 75mm inf guns, 2 x 150mm inf guns.

Total personnel—2589

The motorcycle battalion contained an HQ, 3 rifle coys, an MG coy, and a heavy company, all equipped with the same weapons as the *Panzer Grenadier* battalions but with a total of some 271 motorcycles. Motorcycle combinations were adapted to carry the heavy MGs and the battalion's smaller guns. As with the Panzer Regiment the organisation of the *Schützen* Brigade varied over the years. The brigade came into its own in difficult or close country or where tank obstacles hampered the use of the tanks. As they were equipped with armoured troop carrying vehicles the brigade was able to keep up with

60

Left: Two Sd Kfz 251/7 half tracked personnel carriers leaving a fort in the desert. Capable of carrying nine troops as well as a crew of two these APCs (Armoured Personnel Carriers) were to be found in all Panzer Grenadier battalions. /*Bundesarchiv, Koblenz*

Below: Carrying some of their equipment in a homemade cart, this infantry platoon makes its weary way back from Alamein to Tripoli in Nov/Dec 42. As their greatcoats clearly show it was not always warm in the desert./*IWM*

Top left: The NSU *Kettenkrad*, powered by a small 36hp engine, was used quite extensively in the desert for towing a variety of small loads./*IWM*

Centre left: Infantry soldiers on the march, note the entrenching tools stuck in their belts rather than hanging in the correct place behind their bayonet scabbards. The corporal on the left is carrying a 9mm Pistole 08 Luger pistol holster on his belt as well as what appears to be a captured British Mk II Bren gun. /*Bundesarchiv, Koblenz*

Bottom left: A well laden infantry squad trudge through the sand. They are carrying bed rolls as well as rucksacks, bread bags (*Brotbeutel*) and gas mask canisters. Most also have pith helmets, as well as field caps and steel helmets, so they are equipped for all weathers! /*Bundesarchiv, Koblenz*

the tanks and to fight in close co-operation with them. The motorcycle battalion was particularly flexible and fast moving, suitable for racing the enemy to occupy important features, engaging weak enemy forces, supporting a tank attack (especially by night) by following it up mounted, reinforcing the divisional recce unit and for many other roles. Communication whilst the lorried infantry brigade was on the move was by wireless—a signals platoon of the divisional signal battalion was allotted to the brigade to provide and man these radios—when dismounted they reverted to line.

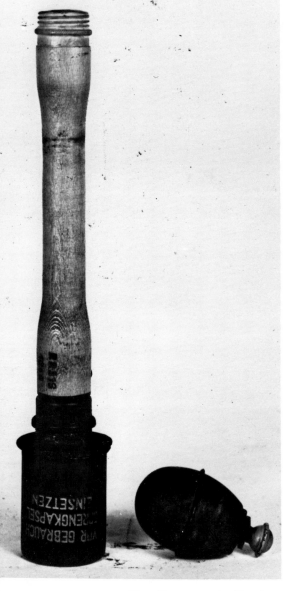

Above: The two standard hand grenades were the HE stick grenade (*Stielgranate* 24) and the HE egg grenade (*Eiergranate* 9). Both had a fuse delay of 4-5 secs. /IWM

Top left: Waiting for Zero Hour. The NCO looking at his watch is armed with an MP 40 sub machine gun, note also the model 24 stick grenade and canvas magazine pouch under his right arm. He is wearing knee length tropical boots and has a makeshift cloth helmet cover on his steel helmet as do the other men in this crowded slit trench./*IWM*

Bottom left: A group of infantry weapons comprising: two standard German rifles (Karabiner 98K)—calibre 7.92mm, effective up to 800m (max 3,000m), weight 9lb, magazine of 5 rounds. An MG 34 machine gun—multi-purpose air cooled 7.92mm calibre, short recoil assisted by muzzle blast, effective range 2,000m and up to 3,500m with telescopic sight (max 5,000m). Also shown are a gasmask and two tin gasmask cannisters (*Tragbuchse*). /*IWM*

Right: An alert sentry with his MG 34 on its bipod mount. /*Col T. Bock*

Below: A light machine gun team with an MG 34 on its bipod mount. The MG 34 had a rate of fire of 800-900 rpm. /*Bundesarchiv, Koblenz*

Left: Twin MG 34 on an anti-aircraft mount (*Zwillingslafette* 34) on the back of a 21 Panzer Division Lorry. /R. *James Bender*/*The National Archives*

Centre right: An optimistic sub machine gunner takes careful aim with his MP 40. Although it had a maximum range of 1,800m its effective range was under 200m. /*Brig P. A. L. Vaux*

Bottom right: An MG 34 on an AA tripod—note the bipod folded back underneath the barrel./*W. Susek*

Left: Examining a captured .45 calibre Thompson sub machine gun, beloved of Al Capone and other Chicago gangsters. The 50 round drum magazine and vertical foregrip show this is one of the earlier Model 1928 A1 type./*Bundesarchiv, Koblenz*

Below: A mortar pit. The mortars are 5cm *leichte Granatwerfer* 36s, the standard German light mortar. It weighed 31lb, max range 570 yards, weight of bomb 2lb, rate of fire 6 rounds in 8 seconds./*IWM*

Left: This *Feldpost* Volkswagen is dwarfed beside an Sd Kfz 251/7 half track.
/R. James Bender/National Archives

Below left: A photographic unit in a Kfz 16 military car, churning up clouds of dust in the soft sand./*Col T. Bock*

Below: A motorcycle (*Kradschützen*) battalion advances through the desert./*Col T. Bock*

Top right: A 105mm howitzer (10.5cm le FH 18) belonging to Artillerie Regiment 190 in action at El Alamein 1942. Werner Susek was the gunlayer of this gun. It was a light field howitzer with a normal maximum range of 11,670 yards which was increased to 13,430 yards by using a more powerful propellant load. To compensate for the increased recoil forces a muzzle break (*Mundungbremse*) was fitted as seen in this picture./*W. Susek*

Bottom right: A 150mm howitzer (15cm 5 FH 18) in a fire position. This was the first type of artillery gun issued to 190 Artillerie Regt in January 1942, but they did not use them in action./*W. Susek*

Artillery Regiment (*Artillerie Regiment*)

There were normally three fully mechanised batteries in an artillery regiment in the Panzer Division. Two were field batteries each consisting of twelve 10.5cm (4.14in) gun howitzers and the third, a medium battery, had either one troop of four 10.5cm guns and two troops each of four 15cm howitzers, or later three troops of the 15cm (5.91in) howitzers. All batteries had light machine guns for local protection and an artillery survey troop was attached to RHQ, for flash spotting and sound ranging. Many other types of artillery guns were used throughout the DAK and the photographs show some of them. Since speed was essential for tank actions, German teaching stressed the need for careful and timely planning on the part of the artillery commander to ensure that his guns would give the most rapid direct support to the tanks and be able to follow their advance as quickly as possible. Close liaison was essential at all levels between commanders and their artillery advisers. In action the commander of the divisonal artillery might move with the CO of the Panzer Regiment in his command tank, or alternatively detach an artillery liaison group to move with the tanks and pass back their requirements. As a rule the two field batteries were detailed for direct support roles and were given priority use of armoured OPs. The medium battery remained under the immediate control of the artillery commander.

Left: A 150mm howitzer under tow by an Sd Kfz 7. It was commonly employed for counter battery fire and had a maximum range of 14,570 yards./*IWM*

Below: A good picture of an 88mm in action (8.8cm Flak 18). Accurate as a sniper's rifle the 88 used in the anti-tank role could easily score a kill at 4,500 yards. It had a 21lb AP shell which would penetrate a 105mm steel plate at 1,000 yards and 30°. /*Bundesarchiv, Koblenz*

Above: A 150mm howitzer under tow by an Sd Kfz 7./*W. Susek*

Centre right: The white rings on the barrel of this 88mm denote tank 'kills' black rings were for soft transport. With a maximum horizontal range of 16,200 yards its devastating accuracy and performance made it one of the most feared weapons of the desert war. It also almost precluded its use in the AA role for which it was originally designed./*IWM*

Bottom right: An 88mm in action. /*IWM*

Far right, top: A Russian gun issued to 190 Artillerie Regiment in April 1942 just before the May offensive. Werner Susek writes, 'We began firing on the British positions on the morning of 27 May, the offensive had begun the day before. The 90th Division started moving at about 2pm. The next day in the morning we were shelled from the left flank. Our infantry attacked but suffered heavy losses. We went into position and opened fire. The British fired back with anti- tank guns, machine guns and field guns. Our battery also had losses, and one of my comrades was hit in the chest by lots of machine gun bullets. Many were injured. However, after about one hour of heavy fighting the British surrendered. Many of their wounded were cared for by our medical officers and then carried back in Sankas (ambulance trucks) to hospital'./*W. Susek*

Far right, bottom: A 7.62mm, ex Russian, field artillery gun in action, June 1942./*IWM*

70

Above and right: 75mm gun belonging to 190 Artillerie Regiment which they never fired in action. It is being towed by an Opel Blitz 1½ ton lorry. The crew was an *Unteroffizier* detachment commander, a gun layer (*Richschütze*), a loader (*Ladekanonier*) and three more gunners./W. Susek

Bottom right: A 15.5cm *Küstengeschütz* in a gun position at Bardia, 26 November 1941. /*Bundesarchiv, Koblenz*

Above: A captured 170mm gun (17cm Kanon 18 in *Mörserlafette*) in Tunisia 1943. It had a maximum range of 29,600m and fired a 150lb shell. /*D. M. Wilkie*

Left: A 170mm heavy artillery gun in action in January 1943. It fired a projectile weighing about 150lb to a maximum range of 32,371 yards./*IWM*

Self-propelled (SP) artillery
The Afrika Korps made increasing use of self-propelled mountings (*Selbstfahrlafetten*) for all types of artillery and it was not long before a self-propelled battalion of eighteen guns was to be found in each artillery regiment in the Panzer division. As the photographs show these were of numerous types, the main ones being the 10.5cm le FH 18 gun mounted on either a PzKw II chassis and called the Wasp (*Wespe*), or on a PzKw 3/4 chassis—the Bumble Bee (*Hummel*). The 105cm le FH 18 was roughly equivalent to a British 25 pounder. It was a very versatile weapon, firing all types of projectiles, including anti-tank (hollow charge).

Far left: A Marder III self propelled gun (Sd Kfz 139 7.62mm Pak 36r). It consisted of the Russian 7.62mm anti-tank gun on an ex-Czech chassis. /W. Susek

Left and below: A Marder II self propelled gun 7.5cm Pak 38r on Pz Kw 38t tank./IWM/Col T. Bock

Above: Marder III. Official designation: *Panzerjäger* 38 *für* 7.62cm Pak 36r (Sd Kfz 139). /FO *Winbourne*

Centre right: A Wasp (*Wespe*). This was a Panzer II chassis mounting a 10.5cm field gun howitzer./*IWM*

Bottom right: A 15cm heavy infantry gun 33 mounted on the hull of a Panzer II. There are six bogie wheels instead of the normal five. It was primarily for close support with a cross country radius of action of 76 miles./*IWM*

Anti-Tank Battalion (Panzjäger—Abteilung (mot))

The battalion consisted of three companies, a light ammunition column of ten lorries and a light supply column of twenty lorries. Each company contained a light platoon of four 3.7cm (1.45in) anti-tank guns, and two medium platoons each with three 5cm (1.97in) anti tank guns. So the total battalion complement was 12 x 3.7cm and 18 x 5cm anti tank guns. Each company had its own transport carrying 1,320 gallons of petrol, baggage and supplies, a workshop lorry, an ammunition lorry and a field kitchen. Because of its cross country speed and mobility the anti-tank battalion was a most useful unit. In defence the average frontage allocated to a platoon was 400m x 400m. In attack they were usually given the task of defending the flanks, however, it was perfectly capable of attacking enemy tanks. As with their other artillery the Germans made increasing use of SP anti-tank guns, the first being the Panzer Jäger 1 4.7cm Pak (t). It was armed with the Czechoslovakian 4.7cm gun.

Above: A 3.7cm anti-tank gun of the 4th Company of 8 Machine Gun Battalion getting ready to withstand a British assault south of Sidi Omar, 18 November 1941./*H. D. Aberger*

Centre right: A 3.7cm anti-tank gun (3.7cm Pak) in position outside a desert fort. It had an effective range of up to 600 yards and could fire 8 to 10 rounds per minute./*Bundesarchiv, Koblenz*

Bottom right: A 2.8cm anti-tank gun (*Schwerpanzebusche* 41). This one was mounted on a captured British truck—note the Afrika Korps palm on rear tail board. /*IWM*

The Anti-Aircraft Battalion (*Flak Abteilung*)
Normally comprised two heavy batteries each of four 8.8cm dual purpose towed guns and one light battery of 2cm and 3.7cm guns. The 88mm was perhaps the most famous anti-tank gun of the war, although it had originally been designed as an anti-aircraft weapon. The Afrika Korps used it almost exclusively in a tank-killing role. It took about two and a half minutes to come into action and 1200 yards was considered its best anti-tank range. The following account was taken from a Middle East training pamphlet published in September 1942 and gives a good example of the anti-tank tactics employed by the Afrika Korps:

'In the Bir Hafid area in summer 1941, one battery of 33 AA Regiment was disposed in an ATk role. The 8.8cm (3.46in) guns attached to the 8th German Tank Regiment accompanied the tanks to within 2,000 yards of our position after we had captured Capuzzo. This group put six of our "I" tanks out of action. The Bir Hafid party was believed to be dug in and was sited in depth behind lighter ATk and field guns. They only came into action after their forward defences had been penetrated; they held their fire until our tanks (a cruiser battalion) appeared on top of the ridge behind which they were sited and then succeeded in knocking out twelve of the sixteen British tanks in the company making the frontal attack. The heavy troop at Halfaya was also covered by lighter weapons and, owing to the compact nature of the defence and natural cover, was able to hold its fire until our tanks were within 600 yards. When this troop came into action all other weapons remained silent. Eleven out of twelve of our "I" tanks were knocked out immediately and, in all, this troop finally inflicted twenty casualties on us".*

* '*Brief Notes on the German Army at War, Supplement No 3—The Artillery in the Armoured Division*'.

78

Below: A 2cm Flak 38 mounted on a three ton Demag D7 semi-track. This gun and vehicle combination was sometimes used in conjunction with 88s to pin down infantry following up behind a tank attack.
/Bundesarchiv, Koblenz

Engineer Battalion (Pioneer—Batallion (mot))
The battalion consisted of two light mechanised companies each of three platoons and a stores troop which carried anti-tank mines, explosives etc; an armoured engineer company of eleven PzKw I and one PzKw II; a mechanised bridging column and a reserve stores park. Their primary task was to keep the division mobile, this included the locating and clearing of obstacles, marking enemy minefields and clearing safe lanes through them, and constructing crossings and bridges capable of carrying all the vehicles of the division. It is also worth noting that both the Panzer Regiment and Panzer Grenadier Regiment had their own integral pioneers.

Above: Engineers clearing a path through a British minefield with a mine detector 22 April 1942. /*Bundesarchiv, Koblenz*

Centre left: An engineer digging a hole to bury a Teller anti-tank mine (on the right, the other mine looks like a British Mk V anti-tank mine). /*Bundesarchiv, Koblenz*

Bottom left: S-mine (*Schrapnellmine*) popularly known as the 'Bouncing Baby', when set off by being stepped on or by trip wires, it jumped about 3-5ft in the air scattering about 350 steel balls in every direction up to 200 yards. /*IWM*

Afrika Korps Tactics

In an account of the operations in Libya during the battles around the Sidi Rezegh area, between 18 November and 27 December 1941, the GOC of 7th Armoured Division (Major General 'Strafer' Gott) made certain observations on the tactics of the Afrika Korps, which I have summarised below:

(a) *Offensive Action.* Before an attack was launched the Afrika Korps would spend the earlier part of the day carrying out a detailed reconnaissance of the area they intended to attack, using armoured cars, tanks and small detachments of infantry. Their main aim was to lure the defence into disclosing its gun positions by engaging these 'baits'. Observation Posts would be watching carefully and any guns which did fire would be pinpointed and subsequently neutralised with heavy fire once the attack began. Their next move was to bring up tanks and anti-tank guns, supported by motorised infantry, to within 2,000 yards of the objective. By this time it was usually midday and replenishment would take place safely, behind a screen of anti-tank guns. At about 1500 hours the attack would be launched. Tanks came forward, supported by very accurate fire from artillery and tanks (usually the heavier PzKw IVs) onto the British field and anti-tank gun positions. A great deal of dust and smoke was caused by this fire in the objective area thus helping to cause confusion among the defenders. In addition, the general direction of attack was usually from out of the setting sun in order to make it more difficult for our gunners to engage targets. Any movement of the defenders' supporting weapons towards the objective was immediately engaged by artillery. The German tanks usually advanced simultaneously at several different points in strong compact formations, their aim being to neutralise the whole area. Tanks then normally engaged in a duel with our artillery and tanks. Whilst this duel was in progress they brought forward their anti-tank guns which were placed on the ground between the German tank positions, and being both effective and inconspicuous, undoubtedly caused us heavy casualties. Whenever possible anti-tank guns were sited amongst derelict vehicles so as to make them even more difficult to spot.

The next phase of the attack took place when one of the tank formations penetrated the objective area, immediately infantry, motoring to within a few hundred yards of their final objectives, followed up with anti-tank guns and automatics. Rapid consolidation took place, with strong all round anti-tank defence. By this time it was usually growing dark and the darkness helped to cover this critical period of consolidation, so there was rarely an opportunity to counter attack the Germans once they had gained an objective. The success achieved with this form of attack was due in no small way to their preponderance of anti-tank guns and the fact that the PzKw III and IV tanks outranged, outgunned and had better vision devices than our cruiser tanks. At the same time, however, this form of attack was costly to the Germans in both men and material.

Below: German gunners from 190 Artillerie Regiment testing a British 25 pounder./*W. Susek*

(b) *Defensive Action and Withdrawal*. The Afrika Korps displayed the same ability to co-ordinate all arms together in defence and withdrawal as they did in attack. Falling back steadily from one prepared position to another, they did not allow themselves to get involved in a running fight. They would offer maximum resistance, but only as long as the positions could be held without risk of defeat, but they were susceptible to any strong threat against their communications. Their overall policy was, sensibly, to save men and material and to sacrifice ground. Having chosen a piece of ground suitable for defence against tanks or assault by a mobile column, they would put out their reconnaissance forces a good deal closer to their anti-tank screen than we would have done. The basis of the defence was their field and anti-tank guns—the latter being well forward as a secure screen, in and behind which were infantry and field guns, within this defensive box there were two forms of mobile reserve —first an anti-tank gun reserve to stiffen up any part of the screen and secondly tanks. The latter were ready for immediate counter attack roles. On occasions, reserve tanks came outside the anti-tank gun screen with the definite intention of luring British tanks onto the screen. Tanks were generally most active in the afternoons.

Withdrawal was from one defensive position to another in two phases. During the first phase they withdrew all administrative vehicles and a proportion of other unarmoured MT. In the second phase tanks moved forward to form a covering screen behind which the remainder of the defence disengaged and mounted. Vehicles formed up in close compact columns and moved off at high speed with the rearguard of tanks still protecting them. Ideally the first phase took place in the dark or under cover of the midday haze. The second phase was nearly always done in the fading light or under cover of early darkness. Whilst acting as rearguard tanks were extremely offensive and, with their superior range, very effective. On at least one occasion they charged British guns in order to give their unarmoured vehicles space in which to disengage.

(c) *Co-operation between Air and Ground forces.* Despite the large degree of Allied air superiority the Germans were, on a few important occasions, able to achieve a high standard of direct air support for their ground troops both by bombing and ground strafing. They operated very close to their own troops both in the offensive and defensive and this led, on occasions, to air attacks on their own forces.

General conclusions from these observations
General Gott went on to draw the following conclusions:

(a) In every phase of battle the Afrika Korps co-ordinated their anti-tank guns, field artillery, infantry and tanks together, working as all-arms teams.

(b) Moves were characterised by speed and compactness. Movement of vehicles was guarded by an outer screen of tanks and an inner screen of anti-tank guns.

(c) Columns were a difficult target for light tank forces to assault, but were vulnerable to air attack and the harassing fire of 'Jock Columns' (These usually consisted of two troops of 25 pounders—their main hitting power—one or two motor companies of mobile infantry, anti-tank and anti-aircraft artillery, a sapper detachment and, for protection, armoured cars and tanks). To overcome this vulnerability frequent long night marches were undertaken.

(d) Their offensive methods were extremely costly and relied little upon manoeuvre. Their method of withdrawal was unlikely to check a determined pursuit for very long which continually threatened their flanks.

Top left: A German forward observation post dug out of the desert sand, March 1942./*IWM*

Bottom left: An advanced observation post, January 1943. /*IWM*

Above: 15cm *Nebelwerfer* (fog thrower) 41 six barrelled rocket launcher. It was used to lay down smoke screens or heavy short range bombardments. The six barrels had to be fired separately to prevent it overturning but this only took 10 seconds./*IWM*

The Desert Fox

So much has been written about Rommel by so many famous and erudite authors, that it would be presumptious of me to imagine that I could magically produce some new and undiscovered facet of that great commander's character. Instead, therefore, I have tried to collect a comprehensive selection of photographs, taken of him at various times during his two years and twentyfive days in North Africa. I hope they will reflect to some degree the tremendous vitality and dedication of this remarkable soldier. It can truthfully be said that he was unique among the senior commanders of the last war in that he was universally respected and admired by both friend and foe alike. Also, he was undoubtedly the highest ranking German officer who retained close contact with ordinary soldiers. He suffered every hardship his men suffered, lived under the same conditions, ate the same food, wore basically the same clothes,

was under the same stress and strain, the same shot and shell, as the humblest private soldier of the Afrika Korps. In addition, he was, as General Westphal once described him, 'the very soul and driving force of the German struggle in North Africa'. Earlier in this book I have given a short resume of his military career. In this section I want to give some idea of what it was like to be with Rommel in the desert. For this reason I have chosen to include a long extract from a book written over twenty five years ago by Heinz Werner Schmidt. Schmidt was one of Rommel's closest companions during the heady days of the first offensive. As a young lieutenant he served Rommel as his personal staff officer, accompanying him on his journeys into the desert to visit his troops and also, on numerous occasions, well into 'No Man's Land'. Heinz Schmidt, who is now living in South Africa, has very kindly

Left: Rommel, in tropical uniform, points authoritatively in the direction of the enemy. Instead of remaining back at his headquarters, he was always in the forefront of the battle, personally influencing events. /*Bundesarchiv, Koblenz*

Below: With battle chaos all around Rommel makes plans, using the mudguard of his staff car as a map rest. /*Bundesarchiv, Koblenz*

Above: Rommel giving orders to 8 Machine Gun Battalion to secure the front at Sollum, 26 November 1941./*H. D. Aberger*

Above right: Greatcoated and sporting a coloured scarf, Rommel consults a map on one of his many recces in April 1942 whilst planning his assault on the Gazala line./*Bundesarchiv, Koblenz*

Right: Rommel's captured British Dorchester ACV (Armoured Command vehicle) called by the Germans a Mammoth (*Mammut*) and nicknamed 'Moritz'. /*R. James Bender/The National Archives*

allowed me to quote from his book. I think that it gives a really vivid impression of Rommel at the height of his prowess. Later of course he was dogged by ill-health, caused mainly by the constant and excessive strain he had put on himself with his ceaseless activity —'He had the strength of a horse', said a young German paratroop officer, himself a skiing champion. 'I never saw another man like him. No need for food, no need for drink, no need for sleep. He could wear out men twenty and thirty years younger. If anything, he was too hard on himself and everyone else'*

General Westphal tells of how during the long retreat on at least two occasions Rommel collapsed unconscious in his arms. The lack of real assistance which he received from Hitler and the Staff in Germany, in particular General Halder, weighed more heavily on him than did perhaps the successes of his enemies in the field.

The goggles

The Rommel legend has been embellished by one or two mundane objects of such tremendous publicity value that one wonders if Rommel had a hidden flair for 'PR' which was just as effective as the more obvious use made

* *Rommel* by Desmond Young.

of it by his great adversary Montgomery. The most famous of these were the British goggles which he wore continuously and how useful they must have been in those dusty, desert conditions. Not quite so well known, but equally useful, were the two large British Dorchester Armoured Command Vehicles which were christened 'Mammoths' by the Germans. In fact they were 'acquired' at the same time as the goggles. Schmidt tells in his book how in April 1941, during the first offensive, a mobile force of motorcyclists intercepted a British column below the Jebel Akhdar and found to their amazement that they had captured two British generals—O'Connor and Neame. The armoured command vehicles belonging to these two generals were also taken at the same time and became known as Mammoths 'Max' and 'Moritz' after characters in a children's story by Wilhelm Busch. After talking to the generals, Rommel, who had made an opportune landing in his Storch aircraft at nearby Mechili airfield, inspected the captured vehicles. Amongst the litter of kit taken out of them was a large pair of sun and sand goggles.

'He immediately took a fancy to them. He grinned and said, "Booty—permissable I take it, even for a general". He adjusted the goggles on the gold braided rim of his cap

Above: Rommel's captured British Dorchester ACV. In addition to the name and the Afrika Korps symbol, it carried on the same mudguard the Korps HQ symbol and a battalion HQ symbol (pennant). /*Bundesarchiv, Koblenz*

peak. Those goggles for ever after were to be the distinguishing insignia of the 'Desert Fox' '.*

Schmidt also relates an incident when Rommel's Mammoth was attacked from the air and the driver badly wounded. Rommel took over the wheel himself and drove all night—I wonder how many other generals would have done the same? For the record Rommel was promoted from Generalleutenant to Generaloberst on 1 February 1942 and to Generalfeldmarschall on 22 June 1942 after the capture of Tobruk. He commanded throughout the campaign apart from two periods of sick leave, the first being in March 1942, when for ten days Generalleutenant Crüwell was acting CO, and again in September—October 1942, when first General der Kavallerie Stumme was in command and then Generalleutenant Ritter von Thoma. Ill health prevented Rommel from remaining in Africa until the bitter end. He left on sick leave on 9 March 1943 never to return and his place was taken by Generaloberst von Arnim who was to make the final surrender on 12 May 1943.

A Front Line Day with Rommel

'Punctually at 7am we leave on one of our customary front line visits. As distances are short, the Mammoth is left at home. In two open cars our party sweeps through the only entrance to Afrika Korps Headquarters, the boom across the road drops behind us again, the sentry salutes. Since Aldinger's going, I travel with Rommel. He sits in front with the driver, I sit behind with Dr Hagemann, the interpreter. We drive past Capuzzo and through a gap in the wire entanglement on the frontier, and rapidly head out in the

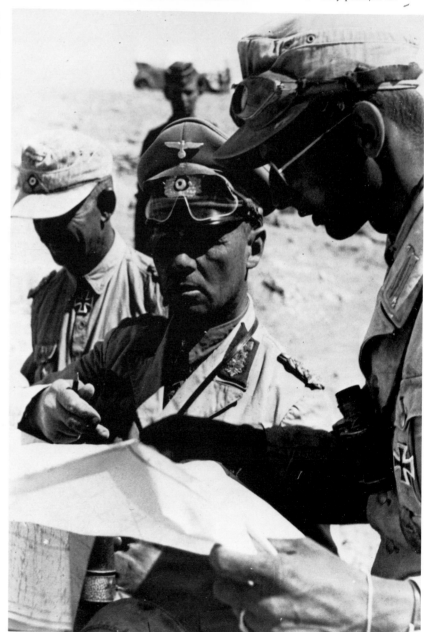

* *With Rommel in the Desert* by H. W. Schmidt.

Desert far beyond our front-line positions. On the horizon in no-man's-land we often spot enemy patrol cars. They cannot guess how fat a prize is moving within eye-shot of their binoculars. Rommel studies our own positions from vantage points on the enemy's side. He examines them through his field-glasses with the painstaking care of a scientist using a microscope. He snorts: he has seen something that displeases him. We leap into the car after him. He stands up as we head straight for the strong-point he has surveyed.

The sentry on duty stares at Rommel wide-eyed. "Why don't you salute?", the General barks. The soldier jumps to attention, petrified, speechless.

"Where is the outpost commander?", Rommel demands angrily.

"He is asleep, Herr...er...Major!" the sentry stutters.

Above: Rommel, wearing an unfamiliar pith helmet, being decorated with the Italian 'Medal for Bravery, by General Garibaldi in front of a parade of Italian soldiers with two M13/40 tanks in the background, 22 April 1941. /*Rommel Museum, Herrlingen*

Right: Rommel presenting an Iron Cross to a member of his staff, 31 August, 1942. /*Bundesarchiv, Koblenz*

Bottom right: Rommel's advanced headquarters near Tobruk, photographed from his Fieseler Storch aircraft./*IWM*

He is a recruit, new to the front, and has not seen Rommel before. The insignia of rank are confusing. He thinks anybody so authoritative must be of field rank: he takes a gamble on 'Major'.

"Ja, Herr Soldat", snaps Rommel. "It seems as if everybody is asleep here. Please wake this—gentleman".

The sentry need not move. The flushed face of a young officer appears at the entrance of a dug-out near by. When he sees the General he comes smartly to attention, salutes and reports:

"Outpost Franke—nothing special to report".

"How do you know, Herr Leutenant?" Rommel raps out at him, "You have been sleeping—and beautifully too".

The lieutenant has nothing to say. There is a grim pause.

Rommel says: "Herr Leutenant, your post is not being run in accordance with my instructions. Your shelter is too prominent. The post is not camouflaged. Your men are running about—while you sleep! I shall return tomorrow and satisfy myself that my requirements are satisfied in every particular. Good morning, Herr Leutenant".

He signs to the driver to start. The young officer stands rooted to the spot. Rommel has gone before he can ejaculate the customary "Jawohl, Herr General". If ever he thought he would find the North African Desert romantic, he has received a rude shock now.

Our cars have been recognised before we reach the next outpost, which is named "Cowa". The strong-point is alert. The lieutenant in command is on the qui vive. Rommel's manner changes completely. But nevertheless he delivers a little homily.

"A well selected position, and good dispositions", he comments. "This is of the utmost important. We cannot take chances. The problem of our supply lines over the Mediterranean make it difficult for us to provide equipment and rations for more troops than we already have in Africa. For this reason we must take the fullest advantage of natural features and whatever else we have at our disposal. One good strong-point must serve as well as two indifferently planned and manned . . . "

"Jawohl, Herr General"

"How are you off for ammunition and supplies?"

"We have plenty of ammunition, Herr General, and food for three days".

"For three days, my friend? You require provisions for three weeks. But . . . never mind, we will see to that".

With a short "Thank you!" Rommel is on his way again.

At every outpost the General leaves his car. Although nearly twice my age he shows no sign of fatigue; my legs are sore and heavy as lead, for it is heavy going in the sand. I make endless notes and write down every request,

Far left, top: Rommel outside his tent near Tobruk. He took pride in being impervious to discomfort and fatigue as his spartan living quarters show. At the age of 50 he was fitter and had more energy than many men twenty or thirty years his junior. /*Bundesarchiv, Koblenz*

Far left, bottom: Rommel talking to Colonel Westphal and staff during a recce. His faithful Fieseler Storch aircraft can be seen in the rear./*Bundesarchiv, Koblenz*

Below: Rommel inside his Fieseler Storch light recce aircraft which he could expertly pilot himself. He was even reputed to have taken off in a raging sand storm during his first desert battle. /*IWM*

every order, every observation. When we get
back it is my duty to bring everything relevant
to the notice of the Chief of Staff or the Chief
Staff Officer. We visit one of our wireless
listening-posts. Two of them are on the
Sollum front, a measured distance apart. They
tune in on the enemy's wavelengths, take
bearings on direction-finding aerials, and, by
triangulation, pinpoint the location of the
enemy's fixed and mobile transmitting stations. The listener at one post reports that
intercepts now indicate that the enemy is
siting his wireless stations northwards towards the sea.

"No wonder", grins Rommel, "in this
weather. Do you imagine that the English
do not like sea-bathing?".

We often visited Halfaya. This day we came
to it after a lengthy tour of out-posts. Captain
Bach, limping with a walking-stick, came up
to meet us. No other officer but Bach was
allowed the privilege of a walking-stick, but
he was no longer young. A pastor in civil
life, he was beloved by his men because of his
considerate treatment of them. In spite of his
unsoldierly profession in peacetime, he ran
his sector more efficiently than many profes-
sional officers ran theirs. Rommel had the
highest regard for him. Halfaya had been the
scene of action before. Rommel recognised
its obvious strategic importance, for it

Far left, top: Tying on a life-jacket, Rommel prepares to fly back to Italy in a Heinkel III. /Bundesarchiv, Koblenz

Far left, bottom: Rommel, pictured here outside his armoured command vehicle 'Moritz' is wearing his leather greatcoat. Only Generals and high ranking officers were permitted to buy these coats. /Bundesarchiv, Koblenz

Above: Rommel talking with Generalmajor von Bismarck, commander of 21 Panzer Division, who was killed by mortar fire 31 August 1942 whilst advancing with the leading battalion of his Division. /Bundesarchiv, Koblenz

Left: Rommel talking with two Italian officers during a visit to one of the Italian Divisions under his command. /Bundesarchiv, Koblenz

Left: Rommel attending an Italian parade. He had little time for the senior Italian officers, but had a paternal way with their soldiers which made him 'simpatico' to them./*IWM*

Below: Probably the most well known photograph of Rommel, it is on sale in postcard size at the Rommel Museum, Herrlingen who kindly allowed me to use it and various other photographs from their collection.
/*Rommel Museum, Herrlingen*

commanded the coast road from Egypt into Cyrenaiça. Denied the road past Sollum and Halfaya, the enemy would be forced far south into the Desert if he aimed at an attack inside Cyrenaica. So Rommel was strengthening this sector as fast as he could, and had just sent to it the elements of the 90th Light that were still immobile through lack of transport.

Bach had just called the company commanders together for a conference. Rommel took the opportunity to give a little talk on tactics.

"Gentlemen", he said, "the struggle in the Desert is best compared with a battle at sea. Whoever has the weapons with the greatest range has the longest arm, exactly as at sea. Whoever has the greater mobility, through efficient motorisation and efficient lines of supply, can by swift action compel his opponent to act according to his wishes. Your troops here at Halfaya Pass are immobile. They are of value against motorised troops only when they are in strong and well-prepared positions, But here again the longest arm has the advantage. We have it—the 88mm gun. It is essential for you, as immobile troops, to have the best-prepared cover, the best camouflage possible, and the best field of fire for the 88's and other pieces".

Rommel paused and then went on, speaking with characteristic forcefulness. "It is my intention to occupy a long defensive line stretching from the sea to Sidi Omar. The outpost positions, up to company strength, must perforce be fairly far apart; but the whole line must be planned in adequate depth towards the rear. Every defended point must be a complete defensive system in itself. Every weapon must be sited so that it is able to fire in every direction. I visualise the ideal arrangement of such defensive points on these lines. One 88mm flak gun should be sunk into the

Left: Colonel Duranti, OC 7 Bersaglieri Regiment (Trento Division) is introduced to General Rommel./*Brig P. A. L. Vaux*

Below left: Rommel briefs one of his staff officers on the route he wishes his recce group to follow. /*Brig P. A. L Vaux*

Below: Rommel pictured during a visit to Recce Battalion AA3. I am told by Col Bock who lent me the photograph that Rommel was telling them that they were not where they had said they were but in a different place entirely— as always he was right!! /*Col T. Bock*

ground as deeply as the field of fire permits. From here trenches should radiate in three directions to three points—one a machine gun position, the second a heavy mortar position, and the third a light 22mm anti-aircraft gun, or to a 50mm pak (anti-tank) gun. Sufficient water, ammunition, and supplies for three weeks must always be available. And every man is to sleep prepared for action".

Rommel warmed to his subject.

"Gentlemen, a few words in regard to battle tactics. In case of enemy attack, the fire of our arms must completely cover the gap between the defended points. Should the enemy succeed in breaking through the gaps, owing to, say, bad visibility, every weapon must be in position to engage towards the rear. Let it be clear that there is no such thing as a 'Direction, Front', but only a 'Direction, Enemy'. He added another pronouncement: "The final decision of any struggle if the enemy attacks will probably rest with the Panzer and motorised units behind the line. Where this decision is reached is immaterial. A battle is won when the enemy is destroyed. Remember one thing—every individual posi-

Above: Rommel is seen here with Hitler and Bormann in Poland. At this time he was a Major General and in command of the *Führerhauptquartier.* Note the cuff title, which was worn by all those army personnel entrusted with the personal safety of the Führer.
/R. James Bender

Centre right: Rommel with the Commander of the 21st Armoured Division, General-major von Bismarck

Bottom right: Rommel discussing the impending attack on Tobruk with a group of young officers. Heinz Werner Schmidt is on the left of the picture, wearing binoculars.
/George G. Harrap & Co. Ltd

tion must hold, regardless of what the general situation appears to be. Our Panzers and motorised formations will not leave you in the lurch, even if you should not see them for weeks . . . I thank you, gentlemen."

The officers were dismissed. Bach accompanied us as we moved on to visit an Italian battery. Here too, Rommel's concern was with ammunition supplies. Dr Hagemann translated the conversations with the Italians; but I noted that Rommel was swift to spot if the translation did not convey precisely the shade of meaning he intended. He knew more Italian than he cared to allow the Italians to perceive. I remember that we were shelled from the east that day as we drove down "Hellfire Pass" towards the coastal plain. The General reckoned that the fire came from self-propelled field-guns which the enemy had temporarily sent forward. On the flat coastal plain Rommel noticed that at some defended points captured British Mark II tanks had been sunk deep in the ground with only their turrets above the surafce. This intelligent employment of enemy material pleased him greatly, and we went on in high good humour.

When we reached the shore, I suggested a dip. We had no bathing-trunks, but who was to worry about that in the Desert front-line? Rommel and I plunged into the cool Mediterranean. It had the lively sparkle of a blue champagne. Rommel splashed about with the gaiety of a schoolboy. The road now led us up the Serpentine Pass towards Sollum Barracks on the escarpment lip. Halfway up we saw sappers blasting a tunnel-like hole into the steep slopes to house an Italian coastal-defence gun. We stopped to examine the work. As usual, Rommel swung round, his glasses probing the hazy east where the enemy lay.

And so, late in the afternoon, back through the boom and into Bardia. No meal all day, but a mass of office work waiting for me. And, for Rommel, the multitudinous tasks that accumulate on paper round even a fighting general.

This, then, was a sample day in my life with Rommel'.*

* 'With Rommel in the Desert' by H. W. Schmidt.

Below: Generalfeldmarschall Rommel being interviewed by a war correspondent, Lutz Koch, who was with him from 1942-44. /R. *James Bender*/*The National Archives*

Rommel Strikes

Der Sperrverband

Rommels's initial orders were to use his newly formed Afrika-Korps as a '*Sperrverband*' (an armoured blocking force) to bolster up the shattered remnants of the once proud Italian army in Tripolitania and prevent further British advances. The idea of them being able to take the offensive was firmly ruled out. Indeed, his Italian compatriots, namely Marshal Graziani, to whom he was in theory subordinate, and General Gariboldi the

Chief of Staff who then took over from Graziani, showed no enthusiasm whatsoever for aggressive action of any kind. It is therefore, a vindication of Rommel's supreme confidence in his own ability to succeed on the battlefield, that a few short weeks later he was able to write home to his wife:

'Dearest Lu,   3 April 1941
  We've been attacking since the 31st with dazzling success. There'll be consternation

amongst our masters in Tripoli and Rome, perhaps in Berlin too. I took the risk against all orders and instructions because the opportunity seemed favourable. No doubt it will all be pronounced good later and they'll all say they'd have done exactly the same in my place. We've already reached our first objective, which we weren't supposed to get to until the end of May. The British are falling over each other to get away. Our casualties small. Booty can't yet be estimated. You will understand that I can't sleep for happiness'.*

Clearly Rommel believed in the old maxim that attack was the best form of defence. He was, however, lucky because, unbeknown to the Germans, the British forces in Cyrenaica had been reduced to a dangerously low level, by the decision to withdraw troops and send them to the assistance of Greece. Cyrenaica was now held by a force of less than two full divisions—the real strength of which lay supposedly in the cruiser tanks of the newly

arrived 2nd Armoured Division. However, large numbers of these tanks were already in workshops and the rest kept breaking down. The division contained only one armoured brigade and only half a support group. They were also 'green' troops, for example, the reconnaissance regiment had only just converted from horses to armoured cars, and none of them had the battle experience of the 7th Armoured Division whose place they had taken. The other division was the 9th Australian which was stronger but still had various deficiences. The widely dispersed and inexperienced British forces would fall easy prey to the advancing panzers.

How impatiently Rommel must have watched and waited as 5 leichte Division landed. Almost before they had found their 'land-legs' or taken a look at their strange new surroundings, than he had their recce forces probing the enemy forward positions. Wolf-

* The Rommel Papers edited by B. H. Liddell Hart.

Below: 1 Coy 8 Machine Gun Battalion on reconnaissance south of El Agheila 24 March 1941. /H. D. Aberger

gang Everth who was commanding an armoured car company in 5 leichte armoured reconnaissance unit (AA3), wrote the following report after taking part in one of their recce missions from 28 February to 1 March 1941:

'On 27 February 1941 I received orders to recce from En Nofilia towards El Agheila on the next day, to take prisoners and if possible to bring back an English armoured car. I reported to my commander at midday on the 28th that I was ready to leave. My recce force consisted of Lt Zeihm's heavy troop. Lt Wolf's light troop. Oberfeldwebel Ludwig's motorcycle troop, an anti-tank platoon from Panzer Jäger Abteilung 39 and a truck from the echelon. At about 1700 hours I reached a position thirty two kilometres east of El Agheila. I at once sent out Zeihm's heavy troop some twenty-one kilometres forward as a protective screen. There it was to remain until it got dark. Around 1730 hours I received a report from Lt Zeihm: "Screen position occupied, abandoned English armoured car near position". I at once sent forward Lt Wolfe in his vehicle, to try to tow the English armoured car. In darkness, at around 1900 hours, Lt Ziehm and Lt Wolf came back and reported that the towing was giving great difficulty and that the vehicle must first be repaired. I now pulled in the anti-tank screen closer to the remainder of the force and then sent Unteroffizier Ruder of the motorcycle recce troop, with three men, twenty one kilometres forward on motorcycles. From there they were to go forward on foot alongside the road (I had ordered gym-shoes to be taken) as far as Kilometre 16, since the English had last been seen there. About half an hour before midnight I heard in the area of my vehicles three shots and cries. When I investigated I found that Rifleman Reichert of No 3 Company, had left his own screen

position for a short time without reporting that he was going out. He had then not halted at the call of the sentries and had been shot by them. At about two in the morning Uffz Ruder came back and reported no enemy up to Kilometre 16, but a minefield on the road at Kilometre 18. I therefore had reveille at five and went forward with Ziehm's heavy troop, two anti-tank guns and a motorcycle section to the minefield. The remainder I left in the rest area under command of Lt Wolf, whom I had recalled. Since the armoured cars could see only poorly by night, I myself went forward on a motorcycle and in the darkness could easily recognise the minefield, which lay on a rise. Since I took it that the English would again have the minefield occupied by day. I took up a position behind the obstacle and waited. In front of me at first light I could see a good six kilometres. Now I brought up Lt Wolf and the remainder of the force, with orders to cover the position occupied previously by Lt Ziehm and simultaneously to get the English armoured car on the road. At around 09.30 hours I saw in the distance two English armoured cars coming towards me. Slowly, continually stopping and observing, they came nearer. About six hundred metres in front of me they stopped again and two men left the vehicles. They came towards us on foot. The vehicles drove around to the south of our positions at a distance of some five hundred metres. When they were exactly opposite us and had seen us I let the two anti-tank guns and one heavy armoured car open fire. Several 2cm shells from the armoured car hit the second vehicle, but unfortunately of the ten shots from anti-tank guns none hit—later it turned out that we had received new 'Tropical ammunition' with different ballistic characteristics and the weapons had not been shot in or adjusted—the enemy vehicles turned and withdrew at

high speed. I took up the pursuit with the eight wheelers, firing further shells from their 2cm weapons which scored hits, but after a cross country chase of about six kilometres the enemy escaped. Now I had the two Englishmen, who had run off into the countryside, picked up. I thus took prisoner a Lieutenant and an NCO. Meanwhile Lt Wolf reported that he had got the English armoured car on the road. My mission was completed. I had taken prisoners and was able to recover an English armoured car. I therefore commenced my long 150 kilometre return march and re-entered the battalion area at around 1700 hours, where my return and reporting to the battalion commander were filmed by a German propaganda company'.

By mid March only 150 tanks had been unloaded in Tripoli harbour of which one third were the light PzKw I s, but Rommel could not curb his impatience any longer. He attacked. El Agheila fell with remarkable ease on 24 March. By the 31st he was attacking the 2nd Armoured Division's positions at Mersa Brega and by 4 April had occupied Benghazi. He now planned to cut straight across Cyrenaica, rather like Seventh Armoured Division had done two months before in order to get behind the retreating Italians. It entailed this time not only crossing two hundred miles of waterless desert, but also struggling through a raging 'ghibli' (sandstorm).

"Rommel's iron will drove them on relentlessly and he made sure that his presence in the front line was known, hovering over them all in his Storch aircraft. Whenever a unit halted for no apparent reason, a note would flutter down from the aircraft to the commander on the spot. It said simply: 'If you do not move on at once, I shall come down. Rommel'.*

* *The North African War* by Warren Tute.

By 11 April the British had been swept in disarray, out of the whole of Cyrenaica, apart from the small force now surrounded in Tobruk, consisting of two Australian brigades and the remnants of 3rd Armoured Brigade, who prepared to defend their already battered stronghold against all comers. But for the remainder it was an ignominious defeat. In just twelve days Rommel had captured all the ground it had taken Wavell fifty to occupy against the Italians.

On to the Frontier!

What was it like to be a member of this victorious force during their gallop to the Egyptian frontier—'The Wire' as it was affectionately called by the British? Here is how it was described in a privately cirulated history of Machine Gun Battalion 8 which was part of 1 Panzer Grenadier Regiment in 5 leichte Division, who had relieved AA3 at El Agheila on 27 March:

'Within the battalion area are other units, ready for the attack on the Mersa el Bregha defile, whose occupation is extremely important for further operations, since a detour round the salt lakes and salt marshes there would only be possible after a great deal of time in entirely unknown terrain.

The 1st April wakes us with artillery fire; so that attack is under way. At about 1400 hours we advance on either side of the road. On the left the unit going ahead of us, Machine Gun Battalion 2, takes Mersa el Bregha after being driven off in the morning. The enemy in front of us withdraws slowly at first, then flees back and by dusk we are 35km east of Mersa el Bregha on the track to Gtafia. Further we can't go as two British batteries pin us down. Motorcycle patrols and Lt Wendland's platoon, reinforced by an anti-tank gun, recce out towards El Gtafia and Bir el Medfun, so we are very well informed about the positions and movements of the opposition.

In the early hours of the next day a British attack spearheaded by armoured cars and carriers is driven off. After a short but effective barrage from our artillery we carry out a mounted attack. Only a minefield laid in front of the British positions lets them get away. By about midday we have approached to within 4km of Agedabia. An attack from the flank is parried by our 5th Company and by No 2 Company of Panzer Jäger Battalion 39. In the follow-up, seventeen armoured cars and six trucks which had bogged down in the sand are captured and thirty crew members taken prisoner. After a short pause the attack continues and two hours later Agedabia and the high ground 4km to its north are taken. General Rommel sends congratulations to our commanding officer on our success.

At about 1800 hours British tanks attack from the area Chor el Bidan. There are perhaps some thirty vehicles, among them Mark IIs, against which our 3.7cm anti-tank gun, (which has earned a reputation for merely rapping at the side of a tank!) is powerless. The situation may become critical. Then Panzer Regiment 5 attacks the enemy in the flank and we witness before us the first tank battle in the desert. In this open country the tanks move in formations reminiscent of war at sea—in line astern and in echelon. Short halt: fire, and continue. Although our tanks are outnumbered they hit seven of the attackers. Our better tactics, the self-reliance of our commanders and our greater mobility are superior to the armoured protection and longer range of the British tanks. After about 45 minutes the battle is over. The burning, smoking hulks of the tanks which have been shot up remain—a ghostly sight in the rapidly falling dusk'.

Now that the British defence was wavering, General Rommel wanted to seize the opportunity of driving the enemy completely out of Cyrenaica. If it were possible to cut off the British retreating north along the coast road, then the majority of the British units would be in a trap. Rommel therefore ordered Operation Ponath. The War Diary of Machine Gun Battalion 8 relates:

'3 April 1941, Agedabia. The difficulties of resupply are giving us considerable trouble. Water still has to be brought from En Nofilia—a 250km round trip. And it's already in short supply there. It comes as no surprise to us when it is ordered that from 4 April the whole Division is to dismount, all trucks and heavy cars are to go back to the Divisional administrative area and are to set up a supply base around Agedabia as quickly as possible. At about 1800 hours all adjutants are ordered to Divisional HQ and there receive detailed orders for this operation. For our own battalion the setting up and command of a special undertaking is ordered, named after our battalion commander, Operation Ponath. The task: with one machine gun company carrying double the normal establishment of weapons, one anti-tank company and one engineer platoon from Hundt's engineer company, to push forward right across the desert via Ghiof el Matar—Bir Ben Gania—El Mechili to Derna and then to block the withdrawal route of the enemy pulling out of northern Cyrenaica. The remaining elements of the battalion are to unload all trucks and will bring up our supplies. It is intended that they should follow up later on the same route. During the night our commander worked out the distance and the endless requirements for water, supplies and fuel. For the operation Nos 1, 2 and 3 Companies are each to provide one machine gun platoon with doubled

weapon complement, but with no increase in personnel. No 1 Company of 39 Anti-tank Unit and one platoon (Lt Krumm's) of No 2 Company, 200 Engineer Battalion have been ordered to come under command. All preparations are made during the night and the force is ready to move at first light. During the morning of 4 April the divisional commander orders two guns from No 2 Battery, 75 Artillery Regiment, to accompany the operation'.

The capture of Derna was seen as being of decisive importance for the further conduct of the campaign which had just started. Here the coast road came down the high plateau of Cyrenaica onto the coastal plain, then through Derna and back up again eastwards on to the Jebel in numerous zigzags. There were no possible detours: on one side was the sea, on the other the deeply scarped Wadi Derna. Just to the east of the zigzags lay Derna airfield which, together with El Adem, was of particular importance both for British resupply and for RAF offensive operations. At 1400 hours on 4 April Operation Ponath finally moved off. The rest of the battalion was to follow under command of Hauptmann Frank with the Division. Let us first stay with the Commander's group. Certainly it was an adventuresome enough operation! Imagine it today: a journey of about 450km over completely unknown desert with vehicles designed for European road and terrain conditions, with maps which proved to be unusable, with insufficient reconnaissance of the ground or of the enemy dispositions, with no desert experience whatsoever—everyone, from Commander to the youngest soldier was taking his life in his two hands.

"The farther one travelled from the coast and into the limitless desert, the higher soared the daytime temperatures which, despite the time of year, approached 50°C. Shortly before dusk set in the area of Ghiof el Matar was reached and there was a short halt so that everyone could sleep and then be briefed on the next stage. Despite the rapid onset of night, Oberstleutnant Ponath continued the march, travelling out in front with his compass and all the rest following in his tracks. In the soft, deep sand however, it was soon impossible to find one's way about and get on, and it became necessary to rest and wait for the morning. At day break we set off anew, after pulling or pushing out those vehicles which had got stuck. Now at last the sandy areas could be recognised and by-passed. Firmer going, on gravel desert, allowed us to move at a faster speed. At around midday the column reached a dried-up well which was probably Bir Bu Hagara. It seemed that the direction of march was correct.

One thing we learned very quickly in Africa; names on the map mean little or nothing. There are no places or prominent features as in Europe. And yet these names, and the little which is concealed in them, are the only aids to getting one's bearings. Names rarely indicate a settlement. Often they refer to a well, which may have dried up or have been filled in by a sandstorm; frequently it is the grave of a pilgrim or a hermit; sometimes just a point where centuries ago stood a settlement long since engulfed by the desert.

After another six hours the Commander's group came to an area which with a great deal of imagination could be made out as the Bir Ben Gania airfield. To the amazement of all, there stood two JU52s and between them General Rommel impatiently awaiting the force. New orders: part of the force was to be air-lifted to El Mechili, to occupy this important post. But the loading soon proved to be in

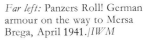

Far left: Panzers Roll! German armour on the way to Mersa Brega, April 1941./*IWM*

Left: A German recce column enters Benghazi, 4 April 1941. /*Keystone Press*

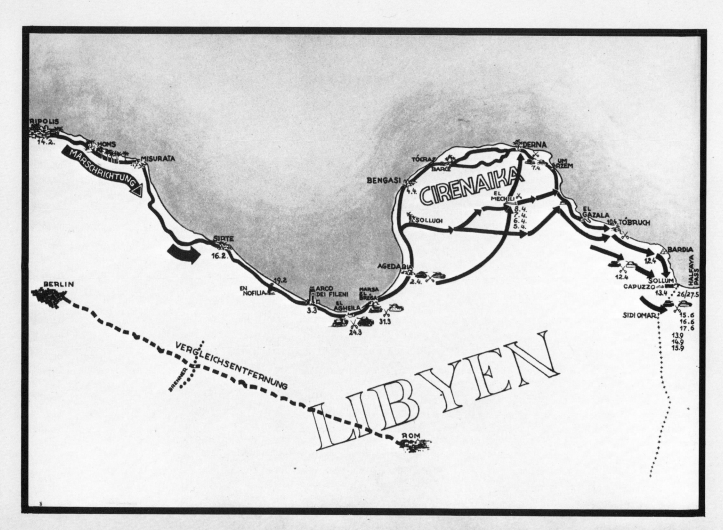

vain; a reconnaissance aircraft landed and reported that El Mechili was occupied by about 3,000 British troops. Unfortunately this interlude cost two hours before the journey could be resumed. About 30km north-eastwards the column came upon a minefield. In spite of careful following of tracks a few vehicles were damaged, but more tragic was the death and injury of several of our comrades.

The 6th of April dawns. The long awaited pause for refuelling and for resting our over-tired drivers is disturbed by a senior officer who pops out of a Fiesler-Storch and orders an immediate resumption of the march at greatest possible speed. Once again the chase across the desert begins and we can only marvel that our vehicles still go through with it. At about 6am a total of six vehicles are still with the Commander about 30km south of El Mechili—all the others have failed to find the RV. A new order over the wireless "Bypass Mechili, and push on to Derna". The question is, whether this little force with its four machine guns and one anti-tank gun can effectively block the road. The Adjutant, Lieut Prahl, dismounts here. He is to collect together the remainder of the force and follow. We travel on and see him standing all on his own in the desert. What if the other groups have got lost? What if an English armoured car appears? We hope we will see him again. In fact he was successful in gathering the force together. General Rom-

mel, who accompanied the advance in his Fiesler-Storch issued him a new order: "Attack El Mechili' ". But during the preparations this order was cancelled and the old cry "On to Derna" was back in force. Where Oberstleutnant Ponath and the leading elements are now we don't know, wireless contact has been lost. Results of reconnaissance passed to us by General Rommel are good. In the area of El Mechili, 3,000 enemy with artillery and tanks; on the track from El Mechili to Tmimi a screen of tanks, armoured cars and artillery. Our stock of fuel is still sufficient for 20km, but water and rations are short. Shortly before we move off a recce sections of two machine gun crews and one anti-tank gun is sent out from our force on Rommel's orders. Under the command of Lt Bukow, it is to block the track near Tmimi. Our little force becomes smaller and smaller; the commander can't be found, some of the vehicles have fallen out and now Bukow's section is detached; Lt Prahl contemplates those remaining with an almost philosophical air. We move on. At about 1600 hours we come up against the British screen. We come under artillery and tank fire. So what—step on the gas and we're through! We make it without casualties, and with the last drop of petrol reach the area of El Ezzeiat. The vehicles are scantily camouflaged in a wadi, the equipment is unloaded and we go forward on foot. Laden with the heavy mountings of the machine guns, with the grenade launchers

Above: Well ahead of his own forward headquarters Rommel surveys the battle at close quarters./*IWM*

Top right: Stoically the garrison of Tobruk went about their household chores even during enemy bombardments./*IWM*

Bottom right: The Afrika Korps continues its successful advance across the desert. /*Bundesarchiv, Koblenz*

and the anti-tank guns there is certainly a hard task in front of us. In spite of this we all have only one goal—the road from Derna.

Suddenly the noise of engines—machine guns and anti-tank guns take up positions—a British convoy is approaching us at moderate speed. If only they'll keep coming towards us! The first truck halts ten metres in front of us. We dash forward and the officer who is dismounting stares dumbfounded into the muzzles of our rifles. Clearly he has taken us for friendly troops and perhaps the German uniform is unknown to him. The British are so surprised that they offer scarcely any resistance. A quick inspection of their vehicles reveals that everything we need is there: petrol, water, rations and as a bonus four officers, 240 men and 40 trucks. We fill up and eat, then continue with our booty acting as an echelon, providing for all our needs. The number of prisoners exceeds our own strength, every other truck carries one of our men travelling as guard.

Unbroken night march—in the morning of 7 April we stop on the track to Derna. Some British fighters circle overhead. The pilots obviously can't make out who has captured who and forbear to press the firing buttons of their machine guns. Soon we are only 9km from Derna. On the side of the track we see another column of about 100 trucks, once again English. We leave our captured echelon behind with a machine gun as guard and drive

up to the column on a broad front. No movement, no defence? When we reach the first vehicle we learn the solution to the mystery; the crews are sleeping peacefully in the cabs and are at first quite exasperated at being disturbed. It takes quite a while before they realise we are German. They obviously haven't expected us so far eastwards. We take another 200 prisoners. Where are we to send this large number? If we take them with us then our force will all be needed as guards. Who will then block the road? If we let them go, then in a short time we'll have the British round our necks. There only remains the possibility of setting fire to their vehicles, destroying their weapons and letting them walk! There is no question of 'abandoning them in the desert'—the walk to the nearest British position is certainly not far. So with a friendly wave they are released. Their expressions range from astounded to disbelieving—they want to stay with us. It needs emphasising with a few cries of "Go on boys!" before they set off.

About 3kms from Derna, quite by chance, we meet up with Oberstleutnant Ponath with his small group in a deep gully, considerably taken up with guarding 200 prisoners of their own, among them two generals. Great excitement on both sides, now we are a fully effective force once again.

What had happened in the intervening time? After the Commander had told the

Adjutant to dismount to gather together the task force, this small band had set off in the direction of Derna. At about that same time there was much racking of brains in the British Headquarters over Rommel's plans. According to Wavell's information the German formations were too weak to be able to go over to the offensive. The extensive reports received all led to a puzzling, though clear, picture: the Germans pushing forward along the coast road to Benghazi. Good, that Wavell had expected. Rommel and his soldiers, inexperienced in desert warfare would not dare to leave the road and go straight across the desert. Yet Germans and Italians were also reported in the area of Msus, and smaller groups were supposed to have been seen near El Mechili and Tmimi. He had no inkling of the wild chase to Derna by Ponath's group.

Only one man saw through Rommel's plan, the Irishman, Major General O'Connor. He, who had commanded the British tank formation in the victorious winter campaign against the Italians was a magnificent leader and a highly intelligent man. He knew that Cyrenaica could become a trap for the British should Rommel reach Derna. On 2 April he flew from Cairo to Derna to assist General Neame, Commander XIII Corps, to

organise the defence in this area. On the same evening that Oberstleutnant Ponath's small group had lost contact with the main body of his task force, that was on 6 April, Neame and O'Connor left Maraua to go to their Headquarters at Tmimi. However, in the darkness their driver overshot the track junction and instead of travelling to Tmimi, drove on further in the direction of Derna. After the past strenuous days the two Generals dozed while a motorcycle patrol from the Commander's group overtook the staff car and stopped it. The English co-driver fired at once and killed one of our soldiers. The second soldier of the patrol fired a burst from his machine carbine—the British driver fell, the Generals raised their hands. When next morning in the PoW area General O'Connor recognised the chief person involved, Feldwebel "Kuttel" Borchardt (No 1 Company), he presented him with his valuable camera with the words "Brave Soldier", but this would not give him pleasure for long, for two weeks later he fell at Tobruk.

So at one fell swoop our Commander's group had captured the two most capable British generals. Just before Derna they had also taken yet another British convoy. However, in attempting to attack Derna airfield at first light with so few men, they were driven off by tanks and armoured cars. And there at about 0930 hours Lieutenant Prahl joined them with the main body of the force, now the reunited task force could continue to carry out its primary task; the blocking of the road and the taking of Derna airfield.

At about 1100 hours we attack and take the northern edge, six RAF transport planes destroyed. We can see a number of fighters on the southern part of this enormous airfield— that is the prize of the day so we think! They shan't have those, think the Tommies. They attack us over the open ground of the airfield with armoured cars and carriers and we are pinned to the ground by machine gun fire. Close combat ensues—hand-grenades against armoured carriers. If a grenade can be lobbed inside the hull, that puts paid to these nippy little desert-bugs. Sometimes this is successful, mostly not. We can't get on, the fighters are able to start up. What a pity! Airworthy fighters captured by a machine gun battalion —that would have been a sensation!

We settle ourselves in on the eastern edge of the airfield and on top of the desert fort south of the coast road. Again and again British columns try to break through to the east—all attempts fail against our concentrated fire. Many turn back, many others give up and are taken prisoner to the deep ravine where our POWs are being held. Our guard of eight men with two machine guns are barely enough to prevent a breakout. But who

would run away in the desert without a vehicle?

A special prize is a British field ambulance and a motorised field workshop. We direct both into the ravine, thereby ensuring that the British and our own wounded are looked after. Germans and British set to work together and the British soldiers help to distribute the captured rations. Together we smoke State Express and Players cigarettes, which to us taste strange.

In these hours comes to each one of us the knowledge that in these conditions the war is being waged under different rules. Here there is no hatred of the enemy; here the only fight is to force one's will on to one's opponent. He who has laid down his weapons is no longer an enemy: he is a Prisoner of War and comes under the protection of the Geneva Convention. The Tommies accept their altered circumstances calmly and with equanimity and their attitude necessitates caution. We speak together in friendly tones but without fraternising. Here on Derna airfield, we discern that the rules of chivalry of former times still apply for the desert war. And it is good that that is so. This will not change in the days to come, this will be the "War without hate".

In the afternoon we attack again and reach the western edge of the airfield. However. we are unable to hold this position against the Mark IIs rolling forward, and we go back to the previous line. As dusk falls the British infantry, with thirty tanks, attack us there. A

Above: 'Business as usual'. Notice outside the Control Office in Tobruk harbour./*IWM*

tough wrestling match ensues, we are able to beat back the infantry but the tanks break through eastwards.

Lacking proper sleep for days we are tired to dropping. But sleep? Scarcely do we close our eyes when infantry fire flares up. Again and again single vehicles and convoys try to break through to the east—in vain, positions hold. The night favours us—it conceals our weakness, lessens our raging thirst and lets us have warning of every noise in good time, but it also conceals from us the strength of the enemy.

At around midnight comes a single car— German or British? We let it come up to our position and then realise that two more English Generals have fallen into our hands. We do not know that with this capture the leading British Generals have all been taken prisoner and only learn this some weeks later.

When we prepare ourselves again for action in the early hours of 8 April, our ammunition state doesn't look too rosy: for each machine gun, only one belt (250 rounds); anti-tank and grenade launcher ammunition all expended, and about 30 rounds of rifle and pistol ammunition is left for each man. In spite of this the action continues almost as if it were a demonstration exercise. Several English and a few vehicles fall into our hands, these are abviously the rest of the airfield personnel. By 0900 we have also occupied Derna, the jewel of Cyrenaica, without meeting any further resistance.

Here is the Africa of our dreams; palm trees, beautiful fragrant flowers in many colours, houses white as snow. Arabs in colourful oriental garments, as well as in bits of Italian and British uniforms, want to sell us eggs, oranges, dates, lemonade and cakes. Other in embroidered slippers, scarves, rings, chains and metal ornaments press against our vehicles. This is the Orient and the "Thousand and One Nights". This splendid oasis is bordered by the deep blue sea—we can almost feel that we are Sinbad the Sailor. The old saying springs to mind; "Here it is good to be, here let us build our dwellings". But it was wartime. A screen was left back in the town and the main body returns to the airfield, whose eastern edge was now occupied facing east. At midday an aircraft circled over the task force—Iron Crosses! After the swastika flag had been laid out the machine landed. We heard from the crew that Task Force Ponath had already been written off as radio communications had never got through. The machine immediately took off again and during the afternoon brought in thirty JU52s. These had ammunition, water and rations on board. Shortly after a flight of Stukas arrived to give cover to the airfield.

At about 2000 hours Rommel arrived and with him the main body of the battalion

Above: Knocked out tanks near Tobruk—the closest is an A13 Mark IIA, the forerunner to the Crusader, belonging to 2nd Armoured Division./*IWM*

which had come via Soluch—Msus—El Mechili. The recce section detached to Tmimi had also returned: unfortunately, though this was to be expected, it had come up against overwhelming British forces and our 3.7mm anti-tank gun could do nothing against tanks, so there were considerable casualties to bewail. In spite of this the remainder, under Lts Bukow and Liesegang, were able to sieze an Indian echelon and bring it with them.

Task Force Ponath generously distributed cigarettes, whisky, gin and corned beef from the captured supplies. It was really time for a victory celebration—however, the Divisional Commander gave the battalion the order to push forward as vanguard of the Division along the coast road to Tmimi. There we were to cut the route of the British escapingthrough El Mechili. In spite of complete lack of knowledge of the terrain or the enemy, the battalion was ready a short time later and moved off eastwards in the darkness".

What then was the result of Task Force Ponath's chase across the desert from Agedabia to Derna? The coast road at Derna was almost completely blocked and 973 prisoners were taken, among them four generals and 176 other officers. One field ambulance, one field workshop, 240 trucks, 36 machine guns and about 400 rifles were captured. About 150 trucks, 6 transport aircraft, 3 carriers, 2 armoured cars and one tank were destroyed.

Tobruk

If ever there was a thorn in Rommel's flesh it was Tobruk. Prewar it had been a small port of some importance, with a population of about 4,000. However, as the harbour was the only safe and accessible port for over 1,000 miles between Sfax in Tunisia and Alexandria in Egypt, apart from Benghazi, it was of great importance to both sides in the campaign. Indeed, as its stubborn defenders held off attack after attack, it assumed an ever growing importance as a morale booster to the British. Rommel had dented their pride severely, if only Tobruk could hold out at least everything was not lost. Typical of the hard fighting which took place around Tobruk is this extract from the diary of a captured German officer of 5 Panzer Regiment, who describes vividly attacks on the stronghold which took place between 11 April and 1 May 1941:

10 April

'Towards evening we reach our advanced positions 17½ miles in front of Tobruk. We have covered 100 miles . . . wearily we pitch camp. Vehicles are checked over. I have to force the louvres open with a hammer, the sand having jammed them; they'll just have to stay open now.

11 April

At 0900 hours we move off into the desert again to the SE in order to cut off Tobruk from the south. With us are anti-tank, machine-gun and anti-aircraft units . . . Ten miles south of Tobruk and already the enemy's artillery is giving us an HE welcome . . . As soon as they get the range we withdraw 100-200 yards. Their fire follows us—their observation must be good. At 1630 hours we attack with two half squadrons. The artillery puts down a barrage, but can make little impression on us. Through! We career on for 1,000 yards and turn carefully through the minefield. As the smoke lifts I see barbed wire and anti-tank trenches.

"Halt!"

Gun flashes.

"Gun, 900. AP shell, light coloured mound, fire!"

A hit. Again—10 yards to the right . . . with six shots we have finished off the anti-tank position. We move along the wire looking for a gap and the leading tank finds one, and in doing so runs on to a mine, of course. Another goes to its rescue, while I give covering fire.

14 April

At 0010 I am called, and ordered to report to the company commander at 0100 hours.

Situation: Machine gunners and engineers have worked a gap through the anti-tank defences; 5 Tank Regiment, 8 Machine Gun Battalion, anti-tank and anti-aircraft artillery will cross the gap under the cover of darkness and overwhelm the positions. Stuka attack at 0645 hours.

0715 hours. Storming of Tobruk. With least possible noise 2 Battalion, Regimental HQ Company, and 1 Battalion move off completely blacked out. Bitterly cold. Of course the enemy recognises us by the noise, and as ill luck will have it, a defective spotlight on one of the cars in front goes on and off.

Soon artillery fire starts up on us, getting the range. The shells explode like fireworks. We travel six miles, every nerve on edge. From time to time isolated groups of soldiers appear—men of 8 Machine Gun Battalion—and then suddenly we are in the gap. Already the tank is nose down in the first trench. The motor whines; I catch a glimpse of the stars through the shutter, then for the second time the tank goes down, extricating itself backwards with a dull thud, with engines grinding.

Below: Victory! The swastika is draped over the shell pocked walls of Fort Capuzzo on the Egyptian border.
/*Rommel Museum, Herrlingen*

We are through and immediately take up file in battle order. In front of us 8 Company, then 2 Battalion HQ Company, then 5 Company. With my troop I travel left of the company commander. With 2 Battalion HQ Company about 60 men of 8 Machine Gun Battalion with Lt Colonel Ponath are marching in scattered groups. Tanks and infantry? —Against all rules! Behind us follow the Regimental HQ Company and 1 Battalion, plus the other arms. Slowly, much too slowly, the column moves forward. We must, of course, regulate our speed by the marching troops, and so the enemy has time to prepare resistance. The more the darkness lifts, the harder the enemy strikes. Destructive fire starts up in front of us now—1—2—3—10—12—16 bursts and more. Five batteries of 25-pounders rain shells on us. 8 Company presses forward to get at them. Our heavy tanks, it is true, fire for all they are worth, so do we all, but the enemy with his superior force and all the tactical advantages of his own territory makes heavy gaps in our ranks.

Wireless "9 o'clock anti-tank gun—5 o'clock, tank!"

We are right in the middle of it with no prospects of getting out. From both flanks AP shells whizz by.

Wireless

"Right turn", "Left turn", "Retire".

Now we come slap into 1 Battalion, which is following us. Some of our tanks are already on fire. The crews call for doctors, who dismount to help in this witches' cauldron. English anti-tank units fall upon us, with the machine guns firing into our midst; but we have no time. My driver, in the thick of it, says, "The engines are no longer running properly, brakes not acting, transmission working only with great difficulty".

We bear off to the right. Anti-tank guns 900 metres distance in the hollow behind and a tank. Behind that in the next dip, 1,000 yards away another tank. How many? I see only the effect of the fire on the terrace-like dispositions of the enemy . . . Above us Italian fighter planes come into the fray. Two of them crash in our midst. The optical instruments covered with dust. Nevertheless, I register several unmistakable hits. A few anti-tank guns are silenced, some enemy tanks are burning. Just then we are hit, and the wireless smashed to bits. Now our communications are cut off. What is more, our ammunition is giving out. I follow the battalion commander. Our attack is fading out. From every side the superior forces of the enemy shoot at us.

"Retire". There is a crash just behind us. The engine and petrol tank are in the rear. The tank must be on fire. I turn round and look through the slit. It is not burning. Our luck is holding. Poor 8th Machine Gunners!

We take a wounded man and two others aboard, and the other tanks do the same. Most of the men have bullet wounds. At its last gasp my tank follows the others, whom we lose from time to time in the clouds of dust. But we have to press on towards the south, as that is the only way through. Good God! Supposing we don't find it? And the engines won't do any more!

Close to our right and left flanks the English shoot into our midst. We are hit in the tracks of our tank, and they creak and groan. The lane is in sight. Everyone hurries towards it. English anti-tank guns shoot into the mass. Our own anti-tank and 8.8cm guns are almost deserted, the crews lying silent beside them. The Italian artillery, which was to have protected our left flank, is equally deserted! English troops run out of their position, some shooting at us with sub-machine guns, some with hands raised. With drawn pistols they are compelled to enter our tanks. The English guns start up and the prisoners fling themselves to the ground. Lieut von Huelsen and my machine gunner lie on that side of my tank which faces towards the MG battalion. We go on. Now comes the gap and the ditch! The driver cannot see a thing for dust, nor I. We drive by instinct.

The tank almost gets stuck in the two ditches blocking the road, but manages to extricate itself with great difficulty, With their last reserves of energy, the crew gets out of range and returns to camp. Examine damage to tank. My men extract an AP shell from the right hand auxiliary petrol tank. The petrol tank was shot away, and the petrol ran out without igniting!

14 April

At 1200 hours we retire into the wadi south of us . . . We cover up. Heavy cumulus clouds cover the sky. Every 10-30 minutes 2 or 3 English bombers swoop out of them amongst the tanks. Every bomber drops 4 to 8 bombs. Explosions all round. It goes on like this until 1900 hours without a pause. The Lion has Wings; we have one, in fact several 'Egons'. These hateful birds immediately direct artillery fire over our post. Likewise smoke bombs, which sail down on parachutes producing a streaming veil . . .

. . . Casualties in 2 Battalion of 5 Tank Regiment, 10 tanks apart from 5 7.5cm guns of 8 Coy! A few dead, several wounded, more missing. The anti-tank units and the light and heavy AA were badly shot up and the 8th Machine Gunners were cut to pieces. The regiment has lost all its doctors—presumably captured. The regiment is practically wiped out.

15 April

Artillery fire from 0700 hours. The bombers repeat yesterday's game.

My troop has two heavy tanks again. Tank No 625 isn't running any more, however. It only serves as a pillbox. According to orders, I report at the brigade commander's office at 1200 hours. Once more the principal subject discussed is the action in front of Tobruk on 14 April. We simply cannot understand how we ever managed to get out again. It is the general opinion that it was the most severely fought battle of the whole war. But what can the English think of us! A weak battalion, only two squadrons strong, bursts through the complex defence system until it is just a mile from the town, shoots everything to bits, engages the enemy on all sides and then gets away again . . .

The war in Africa is quite different from the war in Europe. That is to say, it is absolutely individual. Here there are not the masses of men and material. Nobody and nothing can be concealed. It doesn't matter whether it is a battle between opposing land-forces, or between air-forces, or both; it is the same sort of fighting, face to face, each side thrusting and counter-thrusting. If the struggle was not so brutal, so entirely without rules, you might compare it with the joustings of knights. It was like this at Mersa el Brega, at Agedabia, and now before Tobruk . . .

20 April

In the afternoon tank No 623 rolls up with a new engine. Now I have the strongest squadron in the regiment: 4 PzKw II tanks, 4 PzKw III. Gradually, however, the job of squadron commander is becoming difficult. I have absolutely nothing to go by, everything is in the desert. Where are the tanks, where are the HQ cars, where are A2 and B echelons and squadron office? And I have no command tank and no motorcycle—and then the reports and the paper-war which begins as soon as the last shot has been fired!

23 April

The journey I planned has been postponed

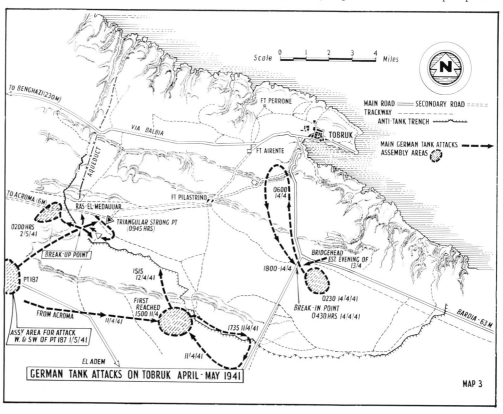

GERMAN TANK ATTACKS ON TOBRUK APRIL-MAY 1941

MAP 3

owing to the arrival of Lieut Grim with 6 tanks, 3 of which belong to our squadron. 621 and 624 are mine—so I change from No 602 back to No 621 again. The engines of the tanks are partly new, partly overhauled in the factory. They have new gears, transmission, brakes etc. The British do not miss the chance of sharing in the welcome with some well-aimed fire. The faithful 625, which is the only heavy tank of the squadron remaining with us, will now be sent back to have its 6 shellwounds. cured. Whilst in the workshop it will have its engines changed.

29 April
50 dive-bombers circling over Tobruk. Tank 622 turns up. They tell us about the desert—of hunger and thirst, of Benghazi and of Derna. Since tank No 625 is still in the workshops, I am getting No 634 as my 5th tank, with Sergeant Schäfer, my driving instructor from Wundsdorf.

30 April
Finishing touches to our preparations for battle. 1745 hours. March to assembly place. Strong Stuka attacks. 2000 hours. Our own strong artillery bombards the enemy heavily. X/105 and X/114 left of us; 8 Machine Gunners in front. 1 Engineer Battalion and 1 Battalion of Assault Pioneers (Sturm-Pioniere) break through and demolish the barriers on either side. The light signals show that the attack has begun. At 2200 hours sleep under the tank.

1 May
We intend to take Tobruk. My 4th attack on the town. Up at 0330 hours, leave at 0430 hours. We lose touch in the darkness and dust—and join up again. We file through the gap where many of our comrades have already fallen. Then we deploy at once, 6 Sqn, on the left, 5 Sqn on the right, behind HQ, 8 and 7 Sqns. The regiment is now Hohmann's Mobile Battalion and consists altogether of 80 tanks.

The English artillery fires on us at once. We attack. No German patrol goes in front to reconnoitre. Tier upon tier of guns boom out from the triangular fortification before us. The two light troops of the company and my left section are detailed off to make a flanking movement. I attack. Wireless message: "Commander of 6 Coy, hit on track".

Then things happen suddenly . . . A frightful crash in front and to the right. Direct hit from artillery shell. No! It must be a mine. Immediately send wireless message: "Commander Schorm on a mine, will try to get old direction".

5 metres back—new detonation. Mine underneath to the left. Now it's all up—with

driving. Wireless message: "Getting back went on mine again".

Now mount tank 623. Back through artillery fire for 100 yards and got in.

Wireless order: "Tanks active behind ridge. The men of the mined tank all right".

Back carefully. Then with the last tank in Company HQ and Lieut Roskoll I give cover to the north. Nine heavy and three light tanks of the squadron have had to give up owing to mines. Of my troop, the commander's tank and both of the section leaders' tanks. Of course the enemy went on shooting at us for some time.

A slight change in position: forward—right—backwards—left! With the commander's approval I am to go up in front to salvage tanks. Whilst we are on the way we are fired at by machine guns and anti-tank guns from about 500 yards. I silence them with HE and drive in the tracks of 624. I bring up the rear, and then the laborious work of salvaging begins. The anti-tank gunfire starts up again, and has to be kept in check by constant fire . . . At last I move slowly off with 624 in tow, through the gap, and on 800 yards. 250,000 Marks saved. The crew is really delighted to have its tank back. Farther on to the battalion. It is now late afternoon.

Dive bombers and twin-engined fighters have been attacking the enemy constantly. In spite of this, the British repeatedly make counter thrusts with tanks. As soon as the planes have gone the artillery starts up furiously. It is beginning to grow dark. Which is friend, which is foe? Shots are being fired all over the place, often on your own troops and on tanks in front on their way back.

Suddenly a wireless message: "British attacking gap with infantry". It is actually true. Two companies get off their motor lorries and extend in battle order. All sorts of light signals go up—green, red, white. The flares hiss down near our MGs. It is already too dark to take aim.

Well, the attack is a failure. The little Fiat-Ansaldos go up in front with flame-throwers in order to clean up the triangle. Long streaks of flame, thick smoke, filthy stink.

We provide cover until 2345 hours, then retire through the gap. It is a mad drive through the dust. At 0300 hours have a snack beside the tank. 24 hours shut up in the tank, with fightful cramp as a result—and a thirst!

2 May
Recovering tanks.
We got out both of the PzKw II tanks . . . 800,000 Reich Marks saved".*

* These extracts appeared as an annexure to a War Office pamphlet entitled *'Periodical Notes on the German Army—German Armoured Tactics in Libya'* which was published in February 1942.

Desert Living

Soldiering in North Africa

'Soldiers in North Africa have different conditions of life to others. How do we live then? Before we went to the base depot to get our new equipment, there were those who were impatient and who wanted to be photographed in their tropical helmets, in photographic studios, because our real surroundings of snow and ice at home didn't go with the equipment. Now, however, our uniforms are grey and bleached like old camel-hair. We have more sand than hair on our heads. We are bronzed, in a word we are old desert campaigners. Our uniform consisted of khaki green breeches and a coat worn open, with a khaki shirt and cravat. I say 'consisted' on purpose, as we don't wear the jacket any more. The shirt sleeves are rolled up and it is bleached with washing, the sun, our sweat and the dew. Our long trousers and breeches stay in our luggage—we only wear short ones. Our high boots are made from a type of canvas, they let the air through and are very flexible. They are laced up and only the bottom part is made of hard brown leather. Even these disappear some days in the heat and soft, easy practical lace up shoes take their place, with green knee length stockings. And because we are vain like all men and for some reason lay particular importance on being brown, we roll our socks down and run around whenever we can, at least half naked or even more so. So one can see us there, tanned and far from home, standing in the morning by the well rubbing the frothing soap over our legs and arms, content with our appearance.

Now to our homes, our tents. They are very practical and easily erected. Everyone has his own small house in which he, of course only stooping, can keep himself to himself. Over the tent roof is stretched an awning. One can imagine the beautiful wind blowing freshly through the tent. In reality the tents are only really useful in the daytime for hatching eggs! Also they must be camouflaged and if we are moving, must be newly erected and newly camouflaged each evening. A trench must be dug, deep and wide enough to take the tent, the roof and sides of which are strewn with sand to absorb the heavy nightly dew. But one must understand this method of erecting a tent, otherwise the sand blows and slides in every possible way and often leaves the occupant no room inside.

Below: This field oven looks large enough to cook a camel!
/Bundesarchiv, Koblenz

One must be able to elude the sand fleas, the snakes and the small yellow scorpions.

If you only find a grumbling chameleon whose peace you have disturbed then excuse yourself politely and wish it goodnight. In the morning, first thing, one shakes ones boots together because scorpions like living in them. Our wash basins are made from impregnated canvas and can be folded together and put in one's pocket. We have two field water bottles which we fill up with our "wonderful" coffee. One cannot drink unboiled water. In the cisterns there are often disagreeable leeches, one has to be careful of them when washing. If we camp near the sea then we bathe in the mornings. Because there are lots of dead salt lakes we have to put up mosquito nets each evening. That our clothes don't get washed very often is obvious. That our provisions consist of anything edible to man is equally obvious. However, something less obvious, if we need tea then we take it from the English!"

That account of soldiering in North Africa appeared in a book called *Balkenkreuz über Wüstensand* which was published in Germany in early 1943. It was clearly written for home consumption and the light, casual style of the article glosses over the realities of living and fighting in that hostile environment. Lt Ralph Ringler, however, was not writing his diary for propaganda purposes, so the joy which he manages to project on the arrival of long awaited food and water rings so much more true to life:

'It is an inexplicable secret how it is possible that suddenly the smoking field kitchen rumbles up. How often had I sworn about Hauptfeldwebel (Regimental Sergeant-Major) Wigl and damned him as a pig and a shirker, but when things got really fiery he was always there at the right time.

"We've got coffee and dried vegetables and there's a bottle of red wine for every four men".

"You are an angel, start getting it out at once because we don't know what will happen in the next half hour."

Another wonder occurred, the sun had only just disappeared into the desert when all at once one of our water wagons appeared. It was hardly possible, this wagon I had sent to El Daba ten days ago and had written it off for certain and now here it was, I felt like embracing the driver. There were six old petrol barrels on board, full of brackish, petrol flavoured, salty, rusty water—and there was rejoicing. Three barrels were immediately given to the field kitchen, one I kept in reserve and the other two I let be distributed amongst the lads. Each man received four litres of this precious liquid—four litres—the first water for a long time. We were invigorated and in high spirits. Now I could watch them—the gluttons, the spendthrifts, the bon viveurs, the thrifty, the happy.

It all depended on the way you decided to use it. First of all a hearty slug, then I washed my face—divine! I put half a litre by for shaving, then I washed my whole body, but none was spilt. A little over a litre remained

Left: Pancakes for supper! Near El Alamein 1941.
/Bundesarchiv, Koblenz

now as a murky soup. Throw it away? Not on your life! Next clothing, first a handkerchief, then my shirt and finally in the thick, dark soup I soaked the tatters of my socks. What a day that was, it had started badly, got even worse, but now this luxury. I came out of it like a man reborn'.

In the same way the following short extract from Wolfgang Everth's diary dispels the impression that the desert is always roasting hot:
'11.1.42. Sunday. Night and morning really lousy cold. Even with three blankets one is frozen like a naked ski instructor. The cold pierces right through everything in the constant wind. One's feet aren't warm until midday. This is no wonder, for how things are in my boots I really don't know at all. The last time I saw my feet was in Brindisi (3.12.41). There are no more changes of socks, so what's the point of taking off a useless pair when I must put them on again'.

Living in the Desert
The photographs in this section will, I hope, portray far better than words the way the Afrika Korps worked, fought, lived, ate, slept and generally conducted themselves in the desert. As you will see they were not all bad times. Soldiers of any army generally manage to make the best of a situation—here for example, is how Wolfgang Everth remembers the first New Year's Eve in the desert:
31.12.41
"In the evening all the reconnaissance troops

came back to the unit. The companies lined up. I gave a review of the past year, remembered the fallen, the wounded and the missing, and ended with a vow of loyalty to the Führer. We listened to the Führer's Order of the Day on the wireless and the greetings from the announcer in Belgrade. Afterwards I was with the CO until shortly before midnight. We drank German champagne from Benghazi. At midnight the bells rang out on the wireless and the German anthem resounded. The whole horizon was full of Verey lights. Every troop sent off every colour, as if there was no war at all. Tracer ammunition blazed into the dark sky and the artillery fired for 5 minutes. After midnight all was quiet and still again. Nothing more was to be heard, only the sound of quiet music coming from the wireless truck. I went round my recce troops—troop leaders, NCOs and men, shaking their hands. We sat for a short time more over a new drink, gin and tinned milk, then it was time for bed; only the footsteps of the sentries could be heard'.

Stranded
One of the most nerve wracking things to happen in the trackless, barren wastes of any desert must be to find oneself stranded, out in the middle of nowhere with the prospect of rescue fading fast. In those circumstances it is only the self reliant who survive. Karl Susenberger tells of just such an occasion:
'Nothing went well in our attack on Tobruk and towards midday on 19 June 1942 the battalion got the order to move in the direc-

117

tion of Bardia. The vehicles were cleaned and off we went eastwards. The journey was more of an armed reconnaissance as we had to be prepared to meet the enemy. Round about Bardia we were especially careful, but the British had already withdrawn. Bardia itself is a small place built right on the coastal cliffs and from there one had a marvellous view of the Mediterranean. We drove up the twisting road in the direction of Capuzzo and reached our predetermined position between Capuzzo and Sidi Omar. Here we rested with the vehicles widely dispersed because we weren't sure whether we would be surprised or not. On the 20 June we heard that Tobruk had fallen. We were greatly overjoyed at the victory and immediately opened a couple of cans of English beer. We were all in good voice and a couple of us were already in Cairo in spirit—but only in spirit. Above all Bernd Rey made a lot of jokes and fun, he was an excellent fellow and a first class friend. On 23 June we got ready again and after the battalion had refuelled we drove further east. About an hour later we passed Sidi Omar and the line of wire that marked the Egyptian border. It was very flat around here and we rolled along without much trouble. We kept a fair distance between each car because the

clouds of sand that rose up made it difficult to follow closely. Sometimes sand got into the car and all this at 50 degrees Centigrade! Finally our car stopped dead, our driver maintained that the engine block had cracked, this was disaster. As Number One Squadron came up Oberschirrmeister (Battalion MT Sergeant-Major) Deitrichsweiler asked what was up, Bernd Rey said that the engine block had cracked.

"Shit!" said Deitrichsweiler "Stay here and at the next stop I'll send someone back to get you".

We were in an awful situation. Our good humour sank below zero. Evening drew on and yet there was nothing to be seen of the breakdown vehicles. I tried to raise Battalion HQ on the radio, but no go. After a while Jochen Grimm tried again—in vain, we were well outside our operating range. In spite of our poor position we still hoped that some vehicle would pass by to help us. Next day we were still hoping—but by evening we had lost the last sparks of hope, especially as we had no map, no compass—nothing. The next day Bernd Rey as the most senior decided that we would spend the day watching and that the next morning we would head for the coast. The rations were divided into four equal

Below: Whilst one man remains on the alert manning the light AA gun, the rest of the crew eat. The bandaged soldier on the right appears to be cooking in a British mess tin, over a blowlamp instead of a stove!/*IWM*

Top right: Tins of AM ('Alter Mann'—literally 'Old Man', also known as 'Mussolini's Backside'!)—A photograph which must stir memories in everyone who fought with the Afrika Korps./*Bundesarchiv, Koblenz*

Bottom right: Eggis for Chai? Bartering in progress—(note soldier on right is carrying a British Penguin paperback!/*Bundesarchiv, Koblenz*

portions; everyone had to give everything up —we didn't know when we would get our next meal. Towards evening we talked it all through again before going to sleep—our only chance was to reach the coast. The next morning as soon as it was light we crawled out of our covering and made everything ready for marching. As water supply we drained the radiator. Finally the built-in radio was destroyed and the vehicle set alight with the rest of the petrol. We marched off leaving the burning vehicle behind us.

We made good progress because the ground was not all sandy. Now and then we paused to conserve our strength. The sun burnt down remorselessly on our heads. The only obstacle we encountered was a sand viper—destroyed by a quick pistol shot. Towards midday we saw a column of vehicles coming towards us. We feared the worst but as they came nearer we saw that it was an Italian column. When they saw us they stopped and a German speaking officer asked what was up. Bernd explained our bad luck and the Italians promised to take us to their unit. We jumped onto a lorry and were glad that this adventure had turned out so well'.

Left: Some people get all the luck—with wine and a white tablecloth! Is the 'waiter' a POW? He is certainly wearing a belt covered with British Army cap badges./*Bundesarchiv, Koblenz*

Right: Afrika Korps soldiers eating a quick snack of captured bully beef and white bread. /*Bundesarchiv, Koblenz*

Below left: A makeshift table on the rear of this vehicle is put to good use. There are some interesting items in the background —including a very posh deck chair!/*Bundesarchiv, Koblenz*

Below, centre: Fresh meat must have provided a wonderful change from the eternal 'Alter Mann'./*Bundesarchiv, Koblenz*

Below right: Fresh fruit! A fairly rare occurrence for Afrika Korps soldiers, certainly during the first four months of the campaign no fresh fruit or vegetables were issued./*Col T. Bock*

Left: A brew up. Waiting for the kettle to boil as a camel train passes by on the skyline./*H. Long*

Below: A water point at work. The 4½ gallon 'Jerricans' were much more robust than their British counterparts. /*Bundesarchiv, Koblenz*

WASSER
AUSGABE

Right: Water bottles were vital pieces of equipment and consisted of the canteen (*Feldflasche*) and cup (*Trinkbecher*). This lucky chap has two canteens!/*W. Susek*

Left: Prosit! Members of 190 Artillerie Regiment celebrating one of the infrequent beer issues —they only got two bottles issued during the whole campaign!/*W. Susek*

Below: Members of 190 Artillerie Regiment take time out for a refreshing drink./*W. Susek*

Above: Spade Drill. Leaving one's shelter with a shovel had special significance!/*Col T. Bock*

Right: A well dug in tent with sand and scrub on top—no wonder the owner is looking so pleased with himself!
/*Col T. Bock*

Above: Men of 1st Battalion Armoured Infantry Regiment 104 (MG 8) doing some cooking near Tarhuna on 14 January 1943 during the withdrawal to Tunisia. /*H. D. Aberger*

Centre left: The HQ of 8 MG Battalion in their position in front of Tobruk in May 1941. (l to r—Comd—Hauptmann Schuette, Adjt—Oberleutnant Prahe, Surgeon—Dr Schmidt.) /*H. D. Aberger*

Bottom left: Digging in at Sidi Omar in early July 1941. /*H. D. Aberger*

Above: A desert bunker with an 'air cushioned' door! Sandbags and earth protect the occupant from bullets and shell splinters. /*Col T. Bock*

Centre right: Sand filled tins and boxes provide the finishing touches to this dug out behind which sits the ubiquitous Volkswagen./*W. Susek*

Bottom right: This field bakery in the middle of the desert produced fresh bread for thousands of soldiers./*Col T. Bock*

Above: Using palm fronds to camouflage tents in a leaguer near Benghazi./*W. Susek*

Centre left: The Operations tent of Recce Bn AA3./*Col T. Bock*

Bottom left: A useful sunshade which was 'acquired' by AA3. /*Col T. Bock*

131

Above: Probably the most novel shelter I have discovered was made out of a knocked out Matilda tank./*IWM*

Right: 'Short back and sides please and not too much off the top'!/*W. Susek*

Far right: When it comes to shaving thank goodness for wing mirrors (yet another use for a Volkswagen!).
/*Bundesarchiv, Koblenz*

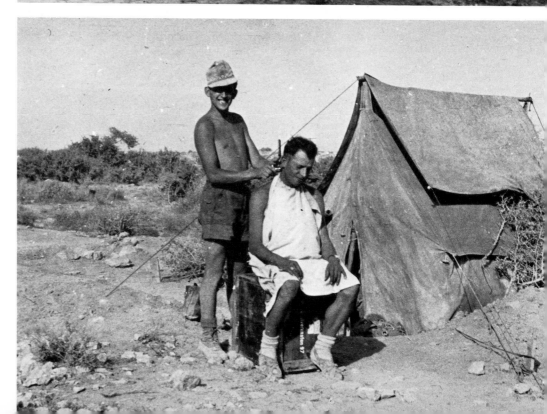

Left: Spit and polish, something every soldier knows all about! */Bundesarchiv, Koblenz*

Below: Sheer luxury! Morning shave by a handy well, with even someone to pull up the water! */IWM*

Top left: Dreaming of home. /*Bundesarchiv, Koblenz*

Centre left: This signpost says it all./*Keystone Press*

Below: More normal military signposts point the way to the kitchen, supply tents etc. of 135 Anti Aircraft Regiment. /*Bundesarchiv, Koblenz*

Above: PT to music helps to keep these newly arrived reinforcements in the pink.
/*Keystone Press*

Right: I hope the needle was sharp! Waiting to be vaccinated, 31 May 1942./*IWM*

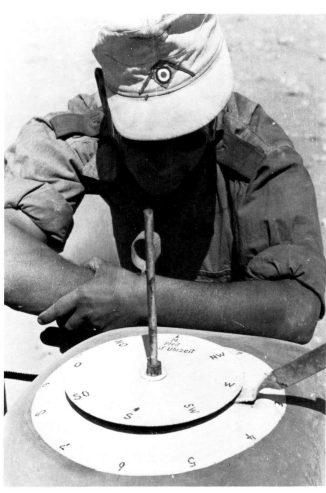

Right: Holy Communion in the desert./*Rommel Museum, Herrlingen*

Below: Cover of the special diary issued to the Afrika Korps for 1942 (Lent by Brig P. A. L. Vaux)./*A. Atkins*

Below right: This page is out of an Afrika Korps diary and deals with protection against the Horned Viper ('wear strong shoes and never go barefoot in the sand. After a bite—immediately tie off the wound and later open it again so that the poison will be washed out with the blood') and the Scorpion ('after a sting, tie off wound immediately, then enlarge it. The only antidote is an injected serum. If possible get remedial medical assistance'). Diary was lent by Brig P. A. L. Vaux)./*A. Atkins*

Far right, top: Desert Mail Call. /*Bundesarchiv, Koblenz*

Far right, bottom: A senior private and his buddy reading mail from home, February 1942 (the truck bears the sign of the Afrika Korps Field Post Office 39). /*IWM*

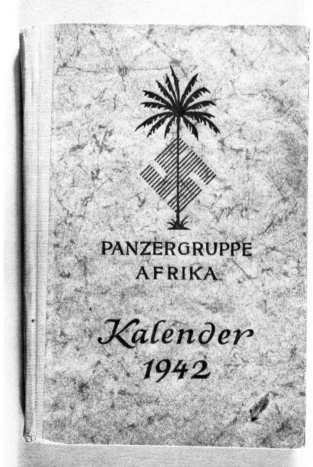

PANZERGRUPPE AFRIKA

Kalender 1942

Hornviper

Länge: 60 bis 75 cm. **Hauptmerkmale:** Über jedem Auge ein stachelhaltiges Horn. Färbung ist der Wüste (ihrer Umgebung) angepaßt. Zeichnung: Auf dem Rücken dunkle braune oder rotbraune viereckige bis rundliche, teils deutlich hervortretende, zuweilen fast verwischte Querflecken, die sich in 6 Längsreihen ordnen und von der Mitte nach den Seiten zu an Größe abnehmen. Vom Auge zum Mundwinkel dunkelbraune Binde. Schuppenreihen verlaufen auf der Rückenmitte in gerader, auf den Seiten in schiefer Richtung. Biß ist gefährlich und kann tödlich verlaufen. Die Hornviper greift den Menschen im allgemeinen nicht an, stößt aber auf bewegliche Gegenstände, die in ihre Nähe kommen. Hält sich im Sande oder an sandhaltigen Orten verborgen, daher nur schwer sichtbar. **Bester Schutz:** Festes Schuhwerk, niemals barfuß im Sande gehen! **Nach einem Biß:** Wunde zunächst gut abbinden und später wieder öffnen, damit das Gift durch das austretende Blut wieder ausgespült wird. (Vgl. Gesundheitsmerkblatt, S. 166.)

Skorpion

Skorpione sind nächtliche Tiere; am Tage halten sie sich unter Steinen, in zerfallenem Holze oder in Erd- und Mauerlöchern verborgen. Sie lieben die Wärme und dringen deshalb gern in menschliche Wohnungen ein. Nahrung: Insekten und Spinnen, die sie mit dem Schwanzstachel töten und dann auskauen und die flüssigen Teile aufsaugen. Der Stich ihres Giftstachels ist sehr schmerzhaft und bei den großen, in den Tropen lebenden Arten (bis 15 cm Länge) selbst für den Menschen tödlich. **Nach einem Stich:** Wunde sofort abbinden und dann erweitern. Einziges Gegenmittel: Serumeinspritzungen. Wenn möglich, sofort ärztliche Hilfe.

SKORPION

23

Left: 'If you know a better 'ole go to it'!/*H. Long*

Right: Sorting out kit on the edge of a foxhole, near El Alamein. /*W. Susek*

Below: Well constructed foxholes in the El Alamein area September 1942./*W. Susek*

Above: Decorations for bravery. Men of 190 Artillerie Regiment receiving Iron Crosses. Lt Schreiber is reading the names and citations./*W. Susek*

Right: Presenting the Iron Cross to a member of Recce Bn AA3. /*Col T. Bock*

Far right, top: General Major Neuman Silkow, Commander of 15 Panzer Division, inspecting a parade of soldiers from Motorcycle Battalion 15 before presenting a Knights Cross (*Ritterkreuz*)./*Brig P. A. L. Vaux*

Far right, bottom: General Major Neuman Silkow, Commander of 15 Panzer Division, presenting a Knights Cross (*Ritterkreuz*). I believe the recipient is Hauptmann Curt Ehle, awarded 28 July 1941. /*Brig P. A. L. Vaux*

Duels in the Sun

'Brevity' and 'Battleaxe'

We left the triumphant Afrika Korps in early May 1941, occupying positions along the Egyptian frontier and putting in a series of unsuccessful attacks upon the stubborn fortress of Tobruk. The remaining months of 1941 saw some of the bloodiest tank battles of the Desert War, before the Afrika Korps was eventually forced to relinquish Cyrenaica completely and retire again to the frontier of Tripolitania. The first British operation, codenamed 'Brevity' began on 15 May, when a composite force under Brigadier 'Strafer' Gott attacked and captured Halfaya Pass. They then advanced as far as Fort Capuzzo, but were counter-attacked by the Afrika Korps and by 27 May had lost the Pass and been forced to withdraw back to where they had started. 'Brevity' was followed in mid June by 'Battleaxe', an equally unsuccessful operation. It was originally to have been mounted with the aims of destroying Rommel's forces and gaining a decisive victory for General Wavell. However, the aims were modified merely to driving the enemy west of Tobruk. This time the Germans managed to hold Halfaya Pass and Rommel once again out-manoeuvred the British, with a wide sweeping counter-attack on the open desert flank to the south. It was Wavell's last offensive and he was replaced shortly afterwards by General Auchlinleck.

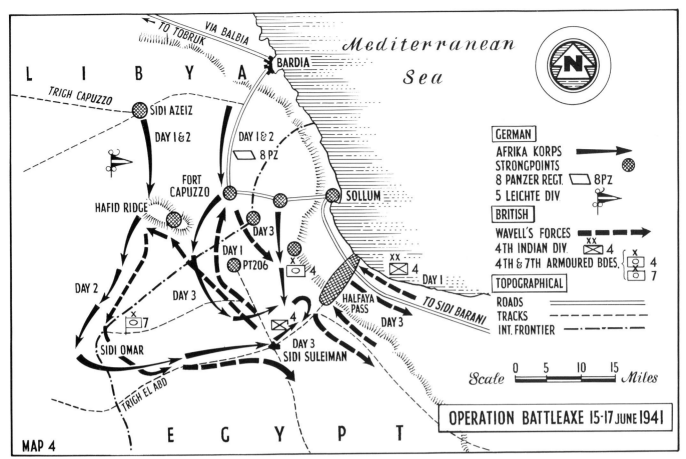

OPERATION BATTLEAXE 15-17 JUNE 1941

MAP 4

Action at Halfaya Pass

To provide the 'muscle' for Gott's 'Brevity' force, 2nd and 4th Royal Tank Regiment had been brought up from Egypt. The Fourth, commanded by Lt Col Walter O'Carroll, with twenty-six Matildas, had to take on the Halfaya Pass position. This is how Lt Peter Vaux (now Brigadier P. A. L. Vaux, OBE, Retd) remembers the action:

'We in the Fourth were engaged in two battles at Halfaya Pass in 1941. The first was Operation Brevity which began on 15 May. 'C' Squadron under Major Miles were to make the actual assault on the German forces at the head of the pass, while 'A' Squadron guarded their flank. I was the reconnaissance and navigating officer in a light tank. The German position was commanded by a Major Bach who was, in fact, a clergyman from Mannheim, but this in no way detracted from his fighting spirit. The attack went in at dawn and by mid morning 'B' Squadron had completely reduced the fortress and the way was clear. 'A' Squadron successfully held off a number of German tanks which had tried to interfere. The attack on the pass itself had been remarkably effective—although the Germans held their very good positions with great courage, they were short of weapons to stand up to the Matilda, although they did knock out seven of them. They withdrew, leaving some 500 prisoners, many dead and a great deal of equipment, especially guns,

145

armoured vehicles, petrol and food. We took a great deal of this away for our own use or intelligence examination and destroyed most of the rest. I personally smashed the radiator of a very nice staff car just before my CO decided to take it for himself—without noticing what I had done. His displeasure when the engine duly seized was not improved by the driver of his own staff car filling up with diesel from a captured jerrican! It was now 'A' Squadron's turn under Major Banks, to lead on to Fort Capuzzo. They had a bad time from German 50mm guns, deployed with typical speed, and many tanks were damaged though none were actually destroyed. We only temporarily occupied the fort and then leaguered for the night at nearby Musaid under a good deal of desultory shellfire. During the night orders were given for our forces to retire and next day we went back to Halfaya. During the day we recovered many of our damaged tanks but some of those further out could not be approached without coming under fire. At dusk I was sent out with my own and another light tank carrying a load of petrol, German anti-tank mines and grenades, with instructions to destroy the tanks we hadn't recovered. On the whole we did so successfully although it was a rather alarming experience, as a dozen German tanks were on the sky line and were apt to fire on us when we got too near. Standing on the turret of one of them was an officer, feet astride and binoculars

trained on us watching the whole operation. Years later, in 1960, when I was commanding the 3rd Royal Tank Regiment in Germany I met this officer again, then adjutant of a battalion in 21 Panzer Brigade and it was fascinating to exchange reminiscences. As we left the scene of our rather sad activities it grew dark, lit only by the tanks we had set on fire, and as we made our way back to Halfaya I saw a German Mark III running parallel to us in the same direction about fifty yards away. Normally my Mark VI light tank could have shown him a clean pair of heels, but the ground was too rough for our short track base to make any speed and I was alarmed that he might blow us to pieces with his big gun for we only had machine guns ourselves. However, he did nothing and after about ten minutes or so drove off into the darkness and was seen no more. I asked the German officer about this and he said to me that his young officer was scared because there were two of us, although he himself had told him that there was nothing to fear from our light tanks. For myself I would be very glad to buy that young officer a drink at any time! Next day 4 RTR withdrew to Mersa Matruh leaving a rearguard under Captain Jim Kendal with myself as guide and radio link. That evening the German tanks went into their old fortress and we slithered away down the rather perilous path to the coast road below, amid scenes of some confusion. As we did so.

Below: A 6.2inch French naval gun, from Tunisia, which Major Bach had managed to obtain to boost up the firepower of his position at Halfaya Pass. /*Brig P. A. L. Vaux*

Top right: This turret of a Matilda, mounting a 2 pounder gun, was set in concrete at Halfaya Pass and used against the British./*Brig P. A. L. Vaux*

Bottom right: A Matilda tank of C Squadron 4th Royal Tank Regiment lies in pieces after receiving several direct hits during the battle on 17 June 1941 at Halfaya Pass. /*Brig P. A. L. Vaux*

Jim—who had already fought in Norway and France, called across from his turret to mine "Peter, why do I always have to take part in military disasters?"

Before I finally got back to the Regiment I had, on the 27 May, my kit shot from off the back of my tank. I had lost it on the same day the previous year at Dunkirk and, incredibly, was to lose it all again, at Gazala, on the 27 May 1942 twelve months later.

Our next visit to Halfaya was as part of the equally ill-fated Operation Battleaxe the following month. By then we had been re-equipped and 'B' Squadron, under Major Clements, had rejoined us from Eritrea. This badly conceived battle was, from our point of view entirely disastrous. 'B' Squadron was again to reduce the pass which once more was held by the redoubtable Major Bach, this time very much on the alert and provided with really powerful anti-tank weapons. Apart from his numerous 5cm anti-tank guns, which were a match for the Matilda at a reasonable range, he had 88mm ack-ack guns, used for the first time in the anti-tank role, and two or three French naval guns of about 150mm, with very long barrels on static mountings. Through someone's incompetence 'C' Squadron were deprived of their pre-dawn approach on the grounds that light was needed for their supporting artillery to see—but the latter never arrived. As a result the Squadron were totally destroyed and many

Above: The end of a heroic defence. The garrison of Halfaya Pass formed up before moving off to a POW camp, 17 January 1942./*Brig P. A. L. Vaux*

Centre right: Graves of the brave crews of C Squadron 4 RTR whose tanks were knocked out during the attack. /*Brig P. A. L. Vaux*

Bottom right: The hero of Halfaya Pass marches proudly into captivity. Major Bach and his RTR escort officer./*IWM*

148

killed including Major Miles—I remember his last wireless message—"These bloody guns are tearing my tanks to pieces".

Much of the same fate befell 'A' Squadron after some initial success, perhaps because two of its troops had been detached in an isolated role on the coast road. These last were also destroyed, but not before Captain Pip Gardner had almost gained the VC he subsequently earned at Tobruk. Possibly things might have gone better had we been permitted to use 'B' Squadron which were being kept in Divisional reserve. In the event it went into action in isolation much later when it too, suffered appallingly, Major Clements being killed. They fought very stoutheartedly, holding up the German tanks for long enough for some of our own forces to escape, Captain Redhead who had taken command, gained the MC for this action—but that is another story. I left the Regiment soon after all this and joined HQ 7 Armoured Division for the November operation (Crusader) from which we returned to Cairo in early 1942. About this time what were called "The German Frontier Force" of Bardia, Sollum and Halfaya, which were now completely isolated, surrendered, and I took a few days leave to go up with my batman and have a look at the German positions. I did not get a chance to speak to Major Bach although I got a photograph of him and the prisoners. I also took a photograph of one of those French naval guns as people who were not there were disinclined to believe they existed. The scene of 'C' Squadron's graveyard was indescribable as may be seen from the photographs. All the German positions were excellently sited with good cover from ground fire and so placed that the tanks were obliged to rear up over stone sangars and expose their vulnerable bellies to the guns. Nevertheless, they had nothing overhead and would have been vulnerable from fire from 'C' Squadron's supporting artillery—had it been there. I do not remember that they had such in the way of mines at the time of our attack—in which case the night approach march which Miles had wanted would probably have succeeded'. Peter Vaux is rightly generous in his praise for the gallant garrison of Halfaya Pass. They did not finally surrender until 17 January 1942, long after the remainder of the Afrika Korps had been forced to withdraw. In the end it was starvation and not enemy pressure which beat them. Their gallant defence was acknowledged by both sides and Major Bach received the Knight's Cross of the Iron Cross for his leadership and personal bravery.

'Crusader'

Both sides spent the summer licking their

Above: The battered frontier post of Fort Capuzzo changed hands many times./*Brig P. A. L. Vaux*

149

wounds and building up their strength for
another onslaught. It came in November,
when Auchinleck launched Operation
Crusader. This included operations to relieve
Tobruk, culminating in the battle of Sidi
Rezegh, in which both sides lost large numbers of their tanks. By the end of November,
although Rommel had won a moral victory
his Afrika Korps was worn out from months
of constant battling and so, on 4 December,
he ordered a general withdrawal. For the rest
of the month the DAK carried out a fighting
withdrawal through Cyrenaica. Typical of the
confused action during those weeks of
December 1941 is this further extract from
Wolfgang Everth's diary. You will remember
that he was a company commander in AA3,
the armoured reconnaissance unit of 5 leichte
Division. He returned to Africa on 5 December 1941 after three weeks home leave in
Germany, knowing nothing of Rommel's
order to withdraw:

5.12.41

Derna. We landed in rain on a completely
soaked, clayey airfield. Ate in the canteen with
Stuka crews who had just returned from a
mission. They knew nothing of the situation,
and had merely bombed their allotted targets
in the desert, attacking convoys there. It is
said here that Rommel has declared "The

situation is favourable". We stood at the roadside and stopped trucks which were travelling to the front, to get them to take us. But all were full of ammunition and petrol. After two hours of gesturing and negotiating in the rain, finally found a truck which was travelling as far as Turimi (90km west of Tobruk). Arrived as dusk fell. Slept the night with a tank regiment's reinforcement company stationed there. The officers there also knew scarcely anything of the situation at the front. They only thought that of my unit not much would be left, for their own regiment had suffered very heavy losses in men and material.

6.12.41

Turimi. In the morning travelled on by lorry. At the roadside signs: "Straggler Collecting Point", and "Reception Command Post". No one knew anything. On the Tobruk ring road I learnt that my unit lay about 40km south, in the desert, but no contact existed with them. However, here I also heard that the echelon was in the neighbourhood. So first I went there and found them in the area of Acroma. Here I found out something of what had happened, as far as the transport was concerned. The transport had been surprised at first light on 22 November from the south. Through a lack of preparation and

vehicle failures many were left there. Vehicles under repair, vehicles which would not start, remained where they were and the rest moved, first from Bardia to the sea and then by night round Tobruk to this place. My own private truck, tent, bed and much else was lost. I reported myself back on the radio link between the echelon and the battalion and learned their exact position. I remained the night here. During the night naval artillery bombarded targets nearby and aircraft attacked the Tobruk ring road with bombs and machine guns by the light of parachute flares.

11.12.41

The recce troops took up new positions in the morning. Water was very short—only $\frac{1}{2}$ litre per man per day. My fitters worked splendidly. The continual breaking of shafts and springs of the armoured cars were put right as quickly as possible. They also had to work for the other companies, whose technical vehicles had broken down. The whole of 4th Company's fitters troop was shot up by Hurricanes, and the Staff Technical Sergeant was killed. In the evening the echelon came up bringing fuel and some water. I received 100 litres for the company but needed 60 litres for the radiators alone. Rations are also short, above all bread. But each vehicle still had tins of English rusks

Top left: Battle commences! Matildas of 4 RTR moving up, note the Afrika Korps panzers on the skyline./*Brig P. A. L. Vaux*

Bottom left: A burning lorry puts up a pall of oily black smoke, silhouetting two knocked out German tanks (Brig Vaux took this photograph only two minutes after the lorry was set on fire). /*Brig P. A. L. Vaux*

Below: Tanks advance! Matildas of 4th Royal Tank Regiment move into battle. /*Brig P. A. L. Vaux*

taken in the previous battle: so to a certain extent all was well. The recce troops remained all night intercepting the enemy wireless nets. Unfortunately have too few recce troops: would like to relieve them. The night was quiet.

16.12.41

The unit was reinforced in the morning by an artillery battery. However, this had only three guns and in all 130 rounds. Our recce troops were pushed back by the English troops. English artillery fire came down on the unit's position. We endured this in our foxholes. I read a 25pf novel. Each time the rounds whistled overhead we put our heads down. A piece of shrapnel hit the wall of my foxhole. When I took hold of it I burned my fingers. Two men were wounded. Then sixty vehicles, including armoured cars, attacked the unit from the south. Those vehicles not absolutely necessary withdrew 6km to the north. The 'F' echelon however, with the artillery and the two 8.8 flak guns held on until evening. The battery had by then fired all but 10 rounds of its ammunition, and moved to join the main

body of the unit, to the north. However, because of the accurate fire of the 8.8s, which shot magnificently in spite of the English artillery fire, the attack was beaten off and the enemy disappeared to the south. A wonder! just before dusk eighteen English armoured cars suddenly attacked the main body of our unit from the north: here there were now no anti-tank guns, no armoured cars, no anti-aircraft guns, for all were engaged against the enemy further south. But now came the artillery—with their last ten rounds and drove off the enemy vehicles to the west. At night the unit took up close leaguer 8km NNE of Signali. All around the noise of engines and light signals, both English and German. Jackals howled dismally nearby. The lack of water is now very serious. No more can be given out for drinking. I issued it in litres and half litres for the radiators.

Below: Rommel in his armoured radio command car (Sd Kfz 250/3) which he named 'Greif' (Strike). It was a familiar sight close to any battle area. A very versatile half track, the 250 had a cross country speed of 37mph, seven forward and three reverse gears./*Bundesarchiv, Koblenz*

Right: The tomb of Sidi Rezegh. Scene of one of the bloodiest battles of the Desert War, both sides fought themselves to a standstill and lost many tanks, guns, vehicles and men.
/Col W. M. S. Jeffery

Below: Close up of a Panzer III with a short barrelled 50mm gun. This looks like the Ausf J which had a ball mounted hull machine gun and thicker armour.
/Bundesarchiv, Koblenz

17.12.41

Moved off at 3 in the morning. Completely dark. The unit moved closed up (5 metres). No lights allowed. Countryside stony and undulating. Very tiring for the crews, who frequently had to go ahead for their vehicles to find good going. Suddenly in front of us an English signal flare and then machine gun fire. Our leading troop fired some 20mm shots. Then complete silence. Engines were switched off. In front of us we could clearly hear English orders and shouts. Then close in front of us the noise of engines, which moved off to the south. It was an English command car troop who had abandoned one vehicle which would not start (1—0 to us!). We continued further. One of my vehicles got both its left hand wheels into a deep hole and turned over. The driver was trapped and only freed after great difficulty. The vehicle had to be dragged upright with one recovery vehicle until it was level and then pulled forward by another vehicle. Thank God nothing was broken. It restarted immediately (German workmanship!). Slowly it became

light. We continued by day. Sandy, flat topped hills of red sand and red rock: past salt lakes, which had to be by-passed. Then later along the Trigh—Engver—Bai, which we mined in a few places. The troops remained all day in contact with the enemy who was following up. South of Mechili we came across a retreating Italian column. They took us for the English and bolted. Only after I had caught up with them in the command vehicle did they quieten down and stop shooting at us. The unit halted 10km SSE of Mechili. Shortly before dark we received some artillery fire from the south. An English bomber force bombed Italian columns near us. German Stukas, which flew southwards over us, got some wild anti-aircraft fire not far to the south. The noise of their bombs was heard loudly. At dusk the armoured car troops arrived after by-passing English columns after it was dark. We should have moved on at 2100 hours, but remained halted. All round were burning vehicles which had been abandoned and blown up so that they should not fall into English hands. The shortage of water

Below: Crews of 4th Royal Tank Regiment and 4th South African Armoured Car Regiment (from the Tobruk garrison) meet at El Duda between Sidi Rezegh and the Tobruk perimeter. This link up was to prove abortive when the Afrika Korps withdrew from the Egyptian frontier and moved westwards to join battle around Sidi Rezegh, 27-29 November 1941./*IWM*

Right: Battlefield scene between Tobruk and Sidi Omar. Panzer IIIs waiting to refuel./*IWM*

Far right: Infantry take a brief rest whilst the artillery continues to hammer away, and the fog of war provides a macabre background to an otherwise peaceful scene./*Associated Press*

Below: The mobility and striking power of the Afrika Korps is exemplified in this graphic photo of tanks, half tracks, and wheeled vehicles of various types, meeting in the desert. /*Bundesarchiv, Koblenz*

Right: A weary member of 8 MG Battalion (Oberleutnant Pfeiffer) after a long night march on foot following the break through at Bir Hagfet Scioma on 1 December 1941./*H. D. Aberger*

Below: The crew of a DR motorcycle combination put their feet up and relax whilst waiting for messages. In the background is an eight wheeled Sd Kfz 231 heavy armoured car and a telephone exchange vehicle Kfz 17./*Budesarchiv, Koblenz*

is now very bad. The armoured car troops who had been in contact the whole day, were very thirsty. Drop by drop the rusty water was given out from the last can and thankfully taken.

18.12.41

0300—false alarm. Back to sleep. 0600 moved to 3km south of Mechili. The English were shooting from the south between our vehicles. English ground attack aircraft attacked with cannon. The unit took up a new position just north of Mechili. Finally got some water from the wells of Mechili. Murky indeed, but what of that. Just drinkable! Also got fuel from the Mechili dump. English bombers came and hurled themselves on the troops pulling back to the west. P.m—the unit pulled out as last troops out of Mechili. The Korps was going straight back down the track to Benghazi. We moved 10km back and to the south as rear screen in the desert. English bombers, which spared us, and German Stukas, passed over us in turn. To the south of us moved the English columns. We could see the sun on their windscreens and on the horizon vehicles with plumes of sand. Very bad going, sandy with washed out wadis. The unit kept going until nightfall. 30km west of Mechili.

19.12.41

0700—Continued to move on the Korp's southern flank. Schnalbe's armoured car troop, which moved out shortly before us, saw an English recce plane making a forced landing The crew set fire to it. A second plane landed alongside. The troop came up to it and fired at it. Unfortunately the machine started up again quickly and escaped through the dust, but the two occupants of the first machine were taken prisoner (two New Zealanders). The move continued through very difficult country, steep hills, deep washed-out stony valleys. In the evening in the area of Charruba. The fitters had to work throughout the night changing the broken springs of the armoured cars and making them fit. No sign of the enemy all day. In the evening a truck came from Korps finally bringing us bread, which had been lacking for days. We had, however, discovered that hunger is easier to endure than thirst'.

So ended another phase of the desert campaign.

Honours Even

And so, after nine months of hard pounding, both sides stood roughly where they had started the previous April, before the Afrika Korps' first impetuous, dazzling advance into Cyrenaica. Both were sadder and wiser. The British had felt the full force of Rommel's first attempt to take Egypt. Next time, and there would undoubtedly be a next time, he might have even greater success. For their part the Germans now knew how much depended upon the tortuous lines of supply across the vast unchartered desert wastes. They were more experienced in the arts of living and fighting in these hostile surroundings. Now they could lick their wounds and rest. Perhaps they might even receive some of the long awaited reinforcements which Hitler and his staff had continually promised them. Next time there would be no stopping them. Tobruk, that thorn in Rommel's flesh, would fall and they would burst irresistibly on the glittering prizes awaiting them in the Canal Zone.

The British too licked their wounds and rested. The great build up would not occur for some time to come. The greatest of all the desert battles was still a dream and 'our friend Rommel' and his Desert Foxes remained a force to be reckoned with. And the general who would perform miracles was still far away in England.

Above: After the battle, wounded British and German soldiers sharing a light./*IWM*